She's On Her Toes

She's On Her Toes

HOW I STARTED A BUSINESS, EXPANDED IT, ALMOST LOST IT, AND GOT BACK ON MY TOES

Carolyn Hern

The Ultimate Guide to Finding Success in the Ultra-Competitive Business of Fitness

ISBN-13: 9781546953937
ISBN-10: 1546953930

Dedication

This book is dedicated to anyone who has fallen down and had the strength to pick themselves up again.

Fall seven, rise eight. –Japanese Proverb

About the Author

Carolyn Hern owns and operates 2 Pure Barre studios in the Winston-Salem area. Between running her studios, managing 20 employees and caring for 3 dogs (2 English Bulldogs and 1 dog that thinks she's a bulldog), she's always on her toes. While Carolyn has an MBA from Wake Forest University, and has worked in politics and investment banking, she has found nothing as challenging as owning and operating her own business.

Carolyn is passionate about her business and leading her team. Throughout the pages of this book and her website www.shesonhertoes.com, Carolyn shares what it's really like to work on her business—you know, all the stuff they don't teach you in business school. You can follow her on Facebook, Instagram, and Twitter at @shesonhertoes.com

Table of Contents

Introduction

There is no better time for a woman to own and operate her own business—especially in fitness. You can't log onto Social Media for more than a nanosecond without glancing at posts followed by #ladyboss, #girlboss, #bossbabe or something similar. It seems like everyone is starting a business and posting away about how amazing their life has become because they are now their own boss and wearing leggings and cute sneakers to the "office."

But are these #legitbosses really #beingboss? Are they running a business? Or is the business running them? This book is a guide to learn aspects of business leadership and management not taught in business school. It shows women in the boutique fitness industry how to attract and hire the right team for their studio as well as how to motivate them to work towards making the business profitable. This book contains strategies and case studies that boutique fitness studio owners can emulate to find success and profitability. If you don't own a fitness studio, don't stop reading now—if you are a women business owner or even thinking of starting your own business, this book is for you. Any of the strategies and case studies discussed can easily be applied across other industries and business models. If you find yourself thinking there is never enough time in the day, then this book is for you too. Keep reading with an open mindset and you will see some radical changes. I know because I was right there with you.

I'll take you through the steps that led me to have the time to write this book. I know you barely have time to eat lunch or write an email, let alone a book. Trust me you'll get the balance in your life that you crave. Let's continue ...

Stepping out of the Shower to Start a Business

Some people recall the morning before their wedding with clarity and fondness. They remember waking up with excitement and anticipation to say "I do" to their one true love; the taste of wedding cake and champagne still fresh on their lips; the song of birds in the air, yada, yada. They enjoy reliving every detail of what was the best day of their life.

For me, that day was the day I decided to take the first steps to start my own business and quit my investment banking job. I got up feeling especially cranky. Took my two English Bulldogs out and fed them (I only had two dogs back then). Got into the shower. And while I was lathering up, inhaling the sweet smell of my shampoo, I realized that I hated my life—correction, I hated my job. I mean, working on all those financial models, pitches and committee memos was literally killing me.

Most of my co-workers were totally clueless. They all thought I was super sarcastic and witty, but really, I was just making fun of them day in and day out. Since they made for easy targets, I'm not necessarily proud of my behavior, but it's not like they were little angels in business suits either.

Our floor had open cubicles and a trading desk. I was one of three women working in the group. Professionalism was at a minimum, to say the least. The guys used to joke that I was going to write down all the off-color, and by-all-definitions sexist things they were saying in a notebook. To say that I was "over it" doesn't even cover the level of frustration I felt. I knew that I was meant for something else besides this "super-supportive" work environment—there's some of that sarcasm and wit!

Working up to 90 hours a week (at my busiest) wasn't fulfilling. Sure, I was making money hand over fist, but I had no time to enjoy it. No time to go out with friends. No time to see my family. For heaven's sake, I had to hire someone to take care of my dogs during the days and evenings. While I did discover how amazing small batch single barrel bourbon tastes, this couldn't possibly be what life is all about. And certainly, there was something better out there for me.

I got out of the shower, dripping wet, in a towel, fired up my laptop and pounded out an email inquiring about opening a Pure Barre studio. For those of you unfamiliar, Pure Barre is a workout that utilizes the ballet barre. Each class incorporates small, isometric movements to amazing heart-pounding music. Your muscles will literally start shaking because they work to their maximum fatigue. And the best part is you can't think about anything else during each hour-long class because you need to be completely focused on the exercises and staying in perfect form.

I love Pure Barre. At the time, it was the only thing keeping me sane. In fact, all of my banking co-workers knew at 10:15 on Saturday morning not to mess with me. I was in class. It was hard to get to class with my work schedule, but I usually went at least twice a week. Sometimes four—that was amazing and meant that I was sleeping at least 5 hours a night.

By 10:00 AM that morning, I had a response from Pure Barre. As I read the requirements for studio ownership, it was like angels floating down from heaven singing. Ahhhh, ahhh. I had enough money to pay the franchise fee and estimated buildout costs (all that investment banking money unspent, locked away in my accounts). I read through the application, filled it out and thought, "I'll keep pursuing this until it doesn't make sense."

Entrepreneur by Accident

I never set out thinking, "I'm going to start a business and work for myself." It just kind of happened. Both of my parents have spent their careers switching back and forth between working for themselves and working for corporations. I grew up seeing them start businesses, sometimes fail at them or realize they weren't going anywhere, or have interests and instincts that led them in another direction. I admire the direction they both took. But I know, now that I've worked for myself, that I can never go back to working for someone else. The freedom to control my own destiny is pretty powerful. And sitting in an office chair that hurts your back is pretty lame.

That being said, if you want to work for yourself because you fantasize about how awesome it would be to wear leggings all day, snap back to reality, because buying a fitness franchise or opening an independent business does not make you a leader. If you're not a leader, you will struggle to manage your team and find business success, life balance and profitability. The good news is that you can learn to be a leader—leadership is a teachable skill.

We've all grown up hearing the phrase "natural-born leader." Sure, some people just have a knack for motivating others and team-building. But even those "natural-born leaders" could benefit from leadership training. The most important thing you can do for your business is invest in yourself and develop your leadership skills.

Unfortunately, leadership isn't taught in business school. I'm sure my professors are violently protesting at reading this, but let's get real. I never attended any classes, lectures or seminars titled, "How to Hire a Rock Star Team and Lead Them to Success." Maybe that was the intent, but it never quite materialized.

We've all read books or heard people give speeches using the following:

"You're only as strong as your team."
"Build a team to build your business."
"You can't do it alone."
"Hire slowly, fire quickly."

Or some version of these.

Sure, that's great to say conceptually, I need to hire a great team. But what gives? How the heck to you find this amazing group of individuals? Do they even exist? Where do you look? What kinds of questions do you ask in an interview? Where is the practical advice on building a team to run your business?

In this book, I'll tell you **how** I hired a Rock Star Team and am currently leading them to success. Like, STEP-BY-STEP. Of course, we have good days and bad, but when I run a sales report at the end of the month, I'm always proud of the work my team has completed. In these pages, you will learn how to find the right team for your business. And even if you are unsure of how to be a leader, you'll learn the steps to transform yourself into an employer your team will be proud of.

Always on My Toes

The title of this book and my blog is "She's on Her Toes," but what does that really mean? According to the Cambridge English Dictionary, "on your toes" means "aware and energetic as a result of being busy and challenged." Sure, it's cute because I own a barre studio, so I'm "on my toes" in class, but being "on your toes" is more than a catchy phrase. It's a methodology of incorporating your business into your already busy life full of commitments to your family, friends, and pets.

Your business is always going to be challenging and keep you busy—it's an entity that is constantly changing and growing. Every day, you'll encounter new problems that require solutions. Some of these "problems" will be fun to solve. How can we create the best possible experience for our clients each and every day? Others not so much so. How can we keep the toilet from backing up each week? It's up to you to be "aware and energetic." In other words, it all starts and finishes with you. You need to be a leader to help your team solve those problems and constantly innovate and improve.

Owning a boutique fitness studio comes with some special business considerations. Just about every boutique fitness studio owner has encountered the following 5 problems:

1. **The perception that making money is "bad" in boutique fitness since making money is often associated with greed, miserly-ness and unjust corporate power—the opposite of the environment we're trying to create for our clients to enjoy when they come to take class or workout.**

2. **Lack of business experience or expertise. Many boutique fitness owners have no formal business training. They love the classes they teach and the studio environment. They are great teachers, but don't know how to run a business.**

3. **Lack of leadership experience. Many owners don't know how to motivate employees or teach them how to sell.**

4. **Most employees are part-time, dis-engaged and lack business savvy. Many boutique fitness employees float from job-to-job and often don't stay at the studio long-term. Keep reading and you will learn how to change that!**

5. **Since teaching and taking class literally requires the owner to work to exhaustion, finding time to work on the business is difficult or limited.**

Whether you own a fitness franchise or operate a unique concept, which you've developed, I'm guessing you can relate to or have experienced 1 or all 5 of these problems. Throughout this book, you will learn how to solve all 5 and create a solid business model which won't compromise the experience you have already created for your clients. In fact, finding solutions to each of these 5 problems will only enhance the client experience you seek to provide and also give you that life-balance you crave.

Are you ready to learn how to stay on your toes? Let's get started!

Part 1: How I Almost Lost My Business: A Lesson in Avoiding Hiring Mistakes

"Somebody once said that in looking for people to hire, you look for three qualities: integrity, intelligence, and energy. And if you don't have the first, the other two will kill you. You think about it; it's true. If you hire somebody without [integrity], you really want them to be dumb and lazy."
–WARREN BUFFET, CHAIRMAN, CEO AND LARGEST SHAREHOLDER OF BERKSHIRE HATHAWAY

"Don't be afraid to fail. You're already super good at it."
–A MEME POSTED ON FACEBOOK BY MY ATTORNEY (HE'S ONE OF THOSE FUNNY ATTORNEYS)

CHAPTER 1

The Definition of a Fitness Business

Before we can get into how you're going to change your business, we first have to define what a fitness business is. There are some unique aspects about owning and operating a business in health and fitness and they open this business model up to some unique challenges that other businesses don't necessarily have to consider. Fortunately, fitness professionals are already highly-motivated and goal-oriented about their health. Now it's time to apply those same principles and disciplines to your business.

It turns out that having a coach is the unspoken secret of the business world. Everyone has one. Correction—every successful CEO, business speaker, hip start-up entrepreneur—they all have a business coach, life coach, speaking coach, thought coach, you name it. Why do they make this investment? It's simple, having a coach makes you work harder.

When I swam competitively, my coach was always pushing me to be better, get more efficient, and work harder. Most importantly, your coach encourages you to push beyond all the crazy limitations you've placed on yourself. You know, the "I can'ts" or the "I've never's." Because you can and you will if you don't doubt yourself and your capabilities.

Wow, so take a second to think. When you are teaching your clients in a class or workout, you are essentially their coach. You're working to push them harder and realize their true potential. Who's doing that for you and your business? If you hear crickets, think about getting yourself a business coach.

When I started working with my business coach, Mary Ann Hauser of ActionCOACH, she explained to me that ActionCOACH defines a business as the following:

Definition of a Business

"A commercial, profitable enterprise that can be run without you."

Does that describe your business? Can you stay home or go on vacation and everything will happen without you? Will the doors be unlocked and clients served? Will you see money deposited into your bank account? If the answer is no, then you own a JOB, not a BUSINESS.

What's so different about a fitness business? When you own and operate a fitness business, specifically, a boutique fitness studio, you aren't just opening your doors every day and selling classes. You are creating a community of like-minded individuals who care about their health and are drawn to your studio because they are looking for your assistance or guidance to keep them fit. They are also more than likely looking for inspiration from you and your team to keep them accountable to this lifestyle—it's really hard to make healthy choices and stick with them. Um, #newyearsresolutionfail anyone?

As the owner of a boutique fitness studio, you don't just own the place, you are a leader or role model to the lifestyle you are promoting.

This brings us to the definition of a fitness business:

Definition of a Fitness Business

A fitness business is a commercial, profitable enterprise that can be run without you so you can be a role model in the health and fitness community you are creating.

Now is the time to get real. As fitness studio owners, many of us lead a double life. We go to our studios every day, yet somehow our daily tasks prevent us time to work out. We appear to be healthy, but behind the scenes, we're not eating good food and not exercising regularly. Does a fitness role model subsist on protein bars, pots of coffee, handfuls of Cheezits, or whatever is convenient? No, they do not.

Do YOU get through the day subsisting on protein bars, pots of coffee, handfuls of Cheezits, or whatever is convenient? Head shakes back and forth—yeah, you know you do.

If your business was able to run without you because you hired a Rock Star team, would you have more time to devote to your health and well-being? Would you be happier and feel more secure running your business? Yes, again!

This is why you want to build your business to work without you. Your team can teach classes, help clients, and sell packages. You need to have more time to devote to being the leader of your fitness community.

There is also a second part to the definition of a business. According to ActionCOACH, not only is your business:

"A commercial, profitable enterprise that can be run without you, this means that you are free to work ON your business not IN it. The business is fully functioning without you."

Unless you are working ON your business, you will never grow your business. This means if you aren't working on the strategies required to have operations, marketing, and financial plans, you'll keep having the same problems and wondering why you aren't living the #bosslady life that you were hoping for. If you don't agree with the definition above, you'll keep having to do everything yourself, make less money, and be miserable while doing it. Definitely not what I signed up for when I opened my studios.

Now some of you are shaking your heads thinking ... "Sure. Sounds great. But how do I get my business to run without me? In my dreams, maybe. I have to be there for everything to happen." Well, guess what? If you don't focus ON your business, you aren't growing your business and it's dying. Yep. That's right. If your business isn't growing it's dying. Everything in life is either growing or dying, including your business and including you. Later in this book, you'll learn how to grow personally as a leader.

Now, if you have just started your business, you might have to do everything yourself in the beginning, but eventually you'll need to hire employees or outsource so you can grow and expand. If you don't plan on growing...then what's the point? Why deal with the stress of owning your own business? Sell now so you can sit on the beach with your toes in the sand.

Once I realized how important it is to hire the right team and give them the responsibility of running my business, then things started falling into place. Hiring the right team is the difference between owning a job and owning a business.

Your goal going forward should be to build your studio based on the definition of a fitness business. In order to be the role model of your fitness community, you'll have to hire a great team and lead them to run the business for you.

Throughout the rest of this book, you'll learn just that. I'll share my experiences that have allowed me to hire my Team, lead them, and then ultimately continue to develop my own leadership skills. It won't be easy to make these changes in your business and yourself, but it will be worth all the effort to turn your business into something that runs without you and gives you more time to spend living a fulfilled life and giving more to family and friends.

It's important to note that managing and leading are two different things. When you manage people, they do what you tell them. When you lead them, they think for themselves. You'll want to commit to developing you and your team's leadership in your business because that is the only way to truly have your business run without you.

But before we get into developing your team and their leader, let me tell you my story of how I almost lost everything.

How to stay on your toes:

In this chapter, we established the definition of a fitness business as the following:

A fitness business is a commercial, profitable enterprise that can be run without you so you can be a role model in the health and fitness community you are creating.

1. *How can you start to make changes in your business so that it will run without you?*
2. *What changes can you make to give yourself more time to work ON your business?*

CHAPTER 2

Hitting Rock Bottom

The owner of 2 successful restaurants in my area once told me that you aren't *really* a business owner until you've fired someone, almost lost all of your money, and been sued. I've managed to accomplish 2 out of 3, so I guess I'm almost there! Goals!

But it's important to understand that if you are struggling with your business and finding it difficult to pay your bills or pay yourself, you are not alone. Every business owner, even the most successful, find business difficult. It ebbs and flows. In fact, business never gets easier, you just get better at it.

I know what you're thinking: "Sure. Easy for you to say. You seem to have all the answers. You don't know what I'm going through to try and hire good people or increase my client base or fill my classes." Possibly not, but before you close this book and use it as a doorstop or fire starter, let me tell you how I hit rock bottom with my business—it could happen to anyone.

It was a cold dark, night. It was raining ... not really but all dramatic stories seem to happen when it's cold, dark, and raining. Actually, hitting rock bottom in my business was something that happened gradually. Until it didn't. And then I started panicking because all of a sudden I realized that I was in trouble and had to make some big changes. I had backed myself into a corner and I was the only one who could fix my mistakes.

What were these mistakes? Well, I ran out of money and managed to rack up some impressive debt, all while increasing sales and having what appeared to be (from the outside) the best year yet for my business. Some of you are thinking: "Oh, a cash flow problem. Yep. Got it." Or you're thinking: "Right, you didn't control your expenses." Worse, I was in the middle of a perfect storm—I had three problems. Cash flow, or the lack of cash at the end of each month, was a problem—correction, a big problem. Expenses were spiraling out of control. And finally, I had a people problem. Specifically, I had a problem with one employee.

At the center of it all was one employee who compounded my cash flow and expense problems to the point that I almost couldn't continue operating my business. Going to the brink of business failure was a terrible experience that I hope to never repeat. No business owner should almost lose everything because of a single employee's reckless behavior. However, the experience did result in me making some incredible changes to my hiring process as well as the daily operation of the studios. These changes are what led me to write this book. Thankfully, I learned how to protect my business and turn it around before it was too late. It all started with defining the values of my business, determining what we are trying to accomplish each day, and establishing what makes our culture unique.

One of the most important things you can do for your business is establish your Vision, Mission and Culture statements so both your clients and employees know what you're all about. I'll talk more about why this is so important as well as how to actually write these statements. But for now, think of the Vision statement as describing the ultimate goal of your business. The Vision statement answers why you are in business in the first place—what drives you to open your doors every day and serve your clients.

Your Vision statement might be such a great goal that you'll always be working towards it. Your Mission statement elaborates on the Vision statement and gives you a mini roadmap of how you and your team plan to accomplish your Vision. And finally, the Culture statement tells your employees what you stand for and gives them a blueprint for all the things that you, as the owner of the business, value in your team.

Unfortunately, I didn't always have my Vision, Mission and Culture statements defined for my studios and when I think back to all of the hiring mistakes I've made (and there have been MANY), it all boiled down to the individual being a bad fit for the studio culture.

That's right. Every bad hire I've ever made didn't fit into our studio culture—specifically these people didn't take class on a regular basis OR EVER. I guess they just didn't care about Pure Barre or value how great our classes are—and that's what made them a terrible fit. I'm not talking about they got busy one week and couldn't fit in class. Or they were sick and decided to get some rest instead of working out. No, these people were never interested in taking class. They just viewed working for me as another job or another paycheck. They had no commitment to our Vision, Mission or Culture and it showed in their behavior.

If you reflect back to any hiring mistakes you've made, I'm willing to bet you would find some similarities. There are likely one or two things that make your business culture unique and the people that didn't excel in your environment likely didn't exhibit those core values.

But back to me and my past mistakes ... Many of my bad hires were just plain clueless. One time, I hired a woman who had worked at another studio in the same role. I thought, "Great. She'll already know what to do, so I won't have to spend too much time training her and answering questions about how to use our client management software." Sadly, I was mistaken. Every time the phone rang, she would answer: "Hello, Pure Barre Chapel Hill." Uh. We're in Winston-Salem. Both are in North Carolina, but that's about it. We got a lot of hang-ups those few months she was there. Head hits desk. Bourbon is poured.

Another time, I was in the car driving out of town for my first vacation since becoming a business owner. A lovely employee called me and told me that she was quitting effective immediately and not coming in that evening so she could go to the beach. And of course, she was scheduled to work all weekend as well. I had to bring the car, full of English Bulldogs, around and back to the studio to finish out the day and cover her shifts that weekend. No vacation for me. Clients were excited to see the dogs in the studio, but if I ever saw her again, I'd really like to explain to her how terrible her work ethic was and that she had absolutely no integrity (while I was envisioning myself punching her in the face).

I've had someone quit before they even started. That was pretty awesome. I'm sure she saved me the time of eventually having to fire her. But seriously?!

My biggest hiring mistake almost cost me both of my studios. I would love to go into specifics, however, I'm sure there are some legal implications to consider. And while I would love to be sued and join the ranks of REAL business owners, maybe I can push that one off a little longer.

Let's just leave it at this: this person thought she knew best. She thought she could create her own schedule and work as many hours has she wanted. Often times she worked beyond a 40-hour work week without permission. She was also reckless with purchasing supplies used in both studios. So yes, I had all three problems previously mentioned. I had a cash flow problem. I had a problem controlling expenses. But at the heart of it all, I had to get this person as far away from my business as possible so I could start fixing the problems she created.

All of these hiring mistakes could have been avoided, if I had simply defined my Vision, Mission and Culture statements. If I knew what I stood for and my business values and culture, then it would have been easier for me to determine the right people to hire to run my business and take care of my clients. The point I'm trying to make is this: if you don't define your business culture and what you want from your employees in each role, you could be one bad hire away from disaster.

Did this person fit our culture? No.

Did she take class? No.

Did she value Pure Barre and see this job as anything more than a paycheck? No.

Did she respect me as the owner of the business and her boss? No.

She never really fit in and that should have been my first sign not to hire her.

But the good news is, if you have defined your business culture, you'll always know the values that you're looking for in a new hire as you're building your team. If someone doesn't match every part of your culture statement, they aren't a good fit and you shouldn't hire them. Defining your studio culture actually makes it easier to find the right employees to enhance your business and take care of your clients.

Maybe you're thinking, I'm desperate to get some help? Someone is better than no one.

DON'T DO IT.

Especially if you're desperate, DON'T DO IT.

This hiring mistake—my biggest hiring mistake—was made under duress. I thought I had to hire someone immediately and it ultimately almost cost me my businesses. I didn't feel good about the decision and that little voice in the back of my head kept saying, "This isn't good. Not liking this situation. She just doesn't seem to fit in." If I had listened to my intuition, perhaps I would have avoided a lot of problems, late night drinking, and lost sleep. And maybe I wouldn't have put my businesses at risk.

Are you scared yet? In truth, YOU, personally can make plenty of other bad decisions to wreck your business—if your business is suffering it's not all about bad hires. But technically, YOU did hire them. Oops.

But back to the topic at hand... Hiring employees needs to be a very deliberate and organized process. If you don't put in the work before the interview to define the role and what you need from your team, that's when problems happen and you make bad hiring decisions. And please listen to your intuition. If you think something is wrong, take a step back and be careful making that hire. In the end, listening to your intuition could save you time, money and lots of exasperation.

I really don't want to end on a sad note and make you think business ownership is hopeless. It's not even close. Please know that things are great with my studios now because I managed to make one really good decision. I took a hard look at what was happening in my business and changed it. I'll explain how throughout the rest of this book.

Think of it this way: If you're struggling, what you're doing isn't working. You need a new perspective. I truly think the sign of an effective leader is the ability to realize when things aren't working, have the courage to change them, and don't look back.

How to stay on your toes:

In this chapter, I explained how making one bad hiring decision almost caused me to lose my business. I also discussed how all of my hiring mistakes were the result of those people not being a good fit for our studio culture.

1. What hiring mistakes have you made in the past?
2. Were there any similarities between these people?
3. Did these people fit in your culture and share your values?
4. Did they value you and your other employees? Or did they alienate your team?

CHAPTER 3

How Did I Get Here? My Butterfly Effect of Avoiding Bankruptcy

New perspective? You're probably asking yourself: "How am I supposed to get a new perspective on my business? I'm sinking here! About to take my last breath because I'm exhausted trying to keep my head above water."

Let's go back to the concept of investing in yourself. That means taking the time to develop your leadership and business skills through courses, podcasts, seminars, webinars etc. But it also means surrounding yourself with good people who are working in your best interest.

I'm not talking about your employees—we'll get into hiring your Rock Star team later. I'm talking about your sounding board—the people that hold you accountable for all the decisions you make in your business. For me, that's 3 people, my financial planner, my accountant, and my business coach.

Have you heard of the Butterfly Effect? The Butterfly Effect is a theory that one small action can have a ripple effect that can dramatically change the course of events and have an impact somewhere into the future. I recently heard Dr. Ivan Misner, Founder of BNI, the world's largest business networking organization, give a speech about The Butterfly Effect and how it's power got him onto Necker Island for a conference with Sir Richard Branson. Dr. Misner was so in awe of how he had arrived at Necker Island to hang out with this group of elite business minds that he actually traced back all of the connections that he had met which got him to his current state of paradise. I'm pretty sure he was also asking himself, "Who the heck was crazy enough to think that I belonged with this group? I'm on Necker Island! Pinch me!" You can read his article here: http://ivanmisner.com/the-butterfly-effect-of-networking/

By asking "How did I get here?", Dr. Misner was able to trace back all of the people he had met or helped, which led him to Necker Island. I'm going to do the same. Unfortunately, the ending is slightly less surreal. I'm going to ask "How did I get here?" to tell you about how I avoided having to file for bankruptcy and thus gained a new perspective on how to operate my business and turn it around. I'm sure both paths ended in cocktails, so at least I've got that going for me.

So how did I get here? Where is "here," anyway? "Here" is owning and operating my business with a great team and not worrying that it's all going to go down in one big blaze of glory. The short answer to how I got "here" is that I hired a business coach, Mary Ann Hauser, with ActionCOACH.

That is how I got a new perspective on running my business and managing my team—from my business coach challenging me to stop sabotaging myself with negative thoughts and remember that I am a leader who can run a great business.

Now you know my business secret. Let me take you through my Butterfly Effect of Avoiding Bankruptcy and learn how I came to meet my business coach.

My Financial Planner & Advisor, Josh Donley, Mosaic Capital

See, the reason I hired Mary Ann to coach me was because I wanted to sell my businesses. I had had enough. As previously discussed, I was having some cash flow issues (although I was not aware of their exact cause at this point) and every month was super stressful to ensure that I had enough money to pay my employees, rent and our other expenses. It literally got down to pennies making sure my accounts weren't overdrawn. Sometimes I couldn't sleep because I was so worried about whether I would have enough money at the end of the month to pay everyone. Sometimes I would get chest pains from the stress.

It seemed like I was just spinning my wheels working to pay American Express. I wasn't having any fun. If that was what business ownership was all about, that was not what I had signed up for. And I was ready to exit.

I was talking everything through with Josh and he said, "This just isn't worth it. You don't need all this stress. You could get a job anywhere, make more money and be less stressed. Let's exit and figure out a way for you to sell." So, he called a business broker, Ron Buck.

Business Broker, Ron Buck, Murphy Business & Financial Corporation

For those of you who aren't aware, a business broker is basically like a real estate agent for businesses. You hire one to help you find a buyer. The broker keeps everything moving and is an intermediary between the seller and the buyer making sure the business valuation makes sense for both parties.

When Josh talked to Ron, he didn't use my name or my business name. Ron was very enthusiastic that he could find a buyer for my business especially because it is a membership-based model with predictable reoccurring revenue and relatively predictable expenses. He suggested a number, which seemed fair. But then he said this: "I mean, it just seems like she's not as profitable as she could be. If she made a few changes and got the business to a little higher level, I could get a much higher number instead of the number I just mentioned." Um, I'm not going to tell you what the numbers were, but let's just say that I wanted the higher one. Like, really wanted the higher one. I was already dreaming of a chair on the beach with a Corona in my hand.

Ron suggested that I talk to this business coach he knew, Mary Ann, who would help me create a plan to exit and get my toes in the sand.

Business Coach, Mary Ann Hauser, ActionCOACH

My first meeting with Mary Ann required a lot of tissues. I was just spent, exhausted, and overwhelmed with all of the "un-fun" things I was having to deal with each day running my businesses. I remember saying, "I have a f**king MBA from Wake Forest. Why can't I make this work? Please help." We talked a little more and as we reached the end of the meeting, she asked me if I was ready to start coaching and how I would like to pay for her services. I had no extra money. I handed her my American Express card and thought: "What do I have to lose? If I don't do this, I'll probably be filing for bankruptcy. If it works, then sweet!"

That is how I got "here." Josh, Ron, Mary Ann. It took the influence of 3 people to help me get a new perspective on how to run my business and turn it around. I don't want you to get the wrong idea here—it took me over 8 months of working non-stop to get my business turned around. It was really hard. In fact, I've never worked harder at anything in my life.

In the beginning, I had a lot of guilt and self-doubt about not recognizing all the harm that one employee was doing to my business. I felt guilty for not intervening sooner. I felt guilty for letting it go that far and putting the business at risk, but it was more than that. I was terribly upset that I put my other employee's jobs at risk—all because I didn't act sooner.

It really messed me up for a while. How could I not have known what she was doing—all right under my nose. Not to worry, I'm out of the blame stage and solidly into the anger stage. Once I was behind her at the dry cleaner's drive-thru pick up lane, and all I kept thinking was: "I just have to push this gas petal." Of course, I didn't. But, damn. That would have been awesome. Oops, my foot slipped. Sorry.

However, to avoid any potential rash acts that might lead to your arrest, now is the time to ask yourself: "How many people will I need to find my new perspective?" Who will you reach out to and set that first meeting to start the process to change your mindset which will then allow you to start changing your business?

It's time to stop struggling and wishing your business was different or better. It's time to be a leader and make it happen.

How to stay on your toes:

In this chapter, I reviewed the Butterfly Effect, a theory that one small action can have a ripple effect that can dramatically change the course of events and have an impact somewhere into the future. Making even one small change can lead to bigger, more profound changes down the road.

1. *What is the Butterfly Effect for where you currently are in your business?*
2. *How many people do you think you'll need to contact to find a new perspective on your business and make changes?*
3. *What is the first step you'll take to start your Butterfly Effect? When will you take it?*

CHAPTER 4

The Unique Challenges of Owning a Boutique Fitness Studio

Now you understand the definition of a fitness business and why it's critical for you to build your business to work without you. As the role model of your fitness community, you've got to have the time to live and promote the lifestyle you are creating at the studio. You need time to support your team and the work they are doing for your studio. Finally, you also need time to come up with the next big idea to "wow" those clients. The fitness world is by definition competitive and your boutique fitness business needs to be ahead of the trends to stay relevant to your clients.

But before we can delve into how you're going to hire this Rock Star team and start making positive changes to your business, it's important to discuss the unique challenges of owning a boutique fitness studio. Once you understand these challenges, you'll be more equipped to transform the job you've created for yourself into a fully functioning fitness business, that runs without you.

Owning a boutique fitness studio comes with some special business considerations. Just about every boutique fitness studio owner has encountered the following 5 problems:

1. The perception that making money is "bad" in boutique fitness since making money is often associated with greed, miserly-ness and unjust corporate power—the opposite of the environment we're trying to create for our clients to enjoy when they come to take class or workout.

2. Lack of business experience or expertise. Many boutique fitness owners have no formal business training. They love the classes they teach and the studio environment. They are great teachers, but don't know how to run a business.

3. Lack of leadership experience. Many owners don't know how to motivate employees or teach them how to sell.

4. Most employees are part-time, dis-engaged and lack business savvy. Many boutique fitness employees float from job-to-job and often don't stay at the studio long-term. Keep reading and you will learn how to change that!

5. Since teaching and taking class literally requires the owner to work to exhaustion, finding time to work on the business is difficult or limited.

I introduced all 5 of these challenges in the Introduction of this book. Oh, you didn't read the Introduction? Or maybe you already forgot these 5 things? Right. Good thing I cut and pasted. Throughout the rest of this book, you'll learn how to overcome all of these challenges.

Are you thinking: "You have an MBA, so tackling these things is easy for you. How am I supposed to address these challenges in my studios with my limited business experience?"

Right back at you. As a fitness expert, aren't you supposed to be open-minded, inclusive, and encouraging? Enacting these changes to your business will require you to be open-minded and you'll need to have a new perspective. You'll need to be willing to make changes. All of these changes will be crafted to improve your business and ultimately help you use your business to let you do more of the things that matter to you like spend time with family and friends, go on vacation, or just get some extra sleep.

Very few concepts discussed in this book are taught in business school. No MBA required to grow a successful fitness business or any business for that matter. I know because I spent over $100,000 to get an MBA and learned almost none of these things until after I had opened my studios.

Why did I shell out for the degree? Remember, before becoming a business owner, I had an investment banking career and an MBA was a requirement for the job. However, three letters don't define a leader or a stellar businessperson. Practical application of basic business concepts will determine your business success and set you apart from your competition. In this book, I discuss the fundamentals of business because you must build a solid foundation before you can do anything else.

Everything discussed in this book is a practical method that anyone can implement or teach themselves. Your success at turning things around all depends how bad you want to change your business? So, how bad do you want it?

How to stay on your toes:

In this chapter, I discussed the unique challenges of owning a boutique fitness studio and revealed that building a solid foundation to your business does not require an MBA or any degree in business—those three letters don't define a leader.

1. *Which of the 5 problems of boutique fitness owner-ship have you encountered?*
2. *Rank each on a scale of 1 to 5 with 1 being "not applicable to you" to 5 being "yes, this is my life, how did you know?"*
3. *What is your biggest business problem right now?*

Part 2: Where are All the Good Employees?

"If you hire people just because they can do a job, they'll work for your money. But if you hire people who believe what you believe, they'll work for you with blood and sweat and tears."
—SIMON SINEK, AUTHOR AND SPEAKER

"It's all about finding and hiring people smarter than you. Getting them to join your business. And giving them good work. Then getting out of their way, and trusting them. You have to get out of the way so you can focus on the bigger vision. That's important. And here's the main thing: you must make them see their work as a **mission***."*
**—RICHARD BRANSON, FOUNDER OF VIRGIN GROUP
(THAT GUY WHO OWNS NECKER ISLAND)**

CHAPTER 5

The Employee Risk Myth

We already touched on the concept that if your business doesn't or can't run without you, that you own a job, not a business. You probably know a lot of people who mistakenly believe they are running businesses, but in fact, just own jobs. The simple fact is: if you are doing everything and nothing happens without your direct input, then you've not yet built a business.

It's important to remember that most businesses all start in a very similar fashion. At the beginning of your business inception, all you have is an idea, a product or service, and you to sell it. In the beginning, it's just you. Eventually, you'll have to grow a team to replace yourself otherwise, you'll risk hitting the maximum threshold of work that only one person can perform and probably physically exhaust yourself in the process.

In business school, hiring more employees to grow your business is called "scaling your company." And don't let anyone fool you. Scaling is just as risky as going into business in the first place. So why risk hiring employees? In the business of fitness, you don't have a choice—you have to scale in order to survive. Let's review the definition of a fitness business:

Definition of a Fitness Business

A fitness business is a commercial, profitable enterprise that can be run without you so you can be a role model in the health and fitness community you are creating.

There is absolutely no way that you can operate a fitness business, teach all the classes yourself, keep up with your clients, manage all of your finances, marketing and all the other daily activities required to keep your studio open without hiring employees.

When I opened my first Pure Barre studio, I was 35. I taught 4 classes each day, oftentimes arrived at the studio before the 6:00 AM class and left after the last class finished at 7:30 PM. When I got home, I kept on working until I just had to get some sleep. I worked on Saturdays and Sundays. I did this for an entire year. It almost killed me.

How focused on my health do you think I was? Not very. In fact, I hurt my shoulder and just kept pushing through it, re-injuring it at least 3 more times. By the time I sought treatment, it took over 2 years and thousands of dollars to fix. How did I hurt myself you ask? Well, I was trying to save $50 by raking my own leaves. Brilliant.

Not having enough employees to help me out was not my smartest move. And while I now have an excuse to never rake leaves again, if I had hired enough teachers in the first place, they could have helped cover my classes while I was recovering from my injury. I probably could have limited my chances for re-injury and recovered faster. Hell, if I wasn't pushing myself working and teaching so much, I might not have even hurt my shoulder in the first place.

Scaling in the fitness world is imperative, otherwise you'll burn yourself out, risk your health and possibly fail at running your business because if something happens to you, you'll be forced to close. But wait you might be thinking, "You just said that scaling was just as risky as going into business. I'll take my chances and go it alone. It's enough risk just to be open in the first place." Let's take a look at the risk involved with scaling. It just might be worth it. Spoiler alert—it is worth it.

It really bothers me when someone brings up the word "risk" in a negative way. Since when did taking a risk turn into something bad? If you Google "risk definition" you'll get "a situation involving exposure to danger." Really? Seems a little extreme.

Starting a business is pretty risky—we've already established that. Ordering day-old sushi involves a degree of risk. Hell, getting married is pretty high up on the risk ladder (there are some really crazy people out there). But are you really putting yourself in harm's way or exposing yourself to danger doing any of these things? Ok, well maybe ordering the sushi. And I am reminded of an amazing story involving a former co-worker, a running vehicle in a home garage and a crazy ex—don't worry, no one was seriously hurt or injured. But, isn't risk just a situation involving a degree of multiple outcomes, or UNCERTAINTY?

As business owners, it's our job to assess risk, by looking at the possible outcomes, developing a plan or strategy to achieve the best outcome and executing that plan—thus mitigating the risk. It's also our job to not freak out if things don't go our way initially. If you're a good leader and manager, you can solve any problem that arises. Or better yet, train your team to solve some of those problems for you.

Taking risks isn't a bad thing. In fact, for small business owners it's a necessity. You took a risk opening your business and now you have to take some risks to grow your business. So why do we seem to put off taking risks?

We over-worry

You know you do it—when you think about taking that one big risk (or even a little one), you start to over-worry about all the things that could go wrong. You start saying things like "I can't, because..." Instead of thinking of risks as dangerous or bad, try thinking about all the opportunities that you might gain. It's easy to focus on the negative side of risk. But what about all the positives that come from risk-taking? Oh yeah, those.

We jump straight to "No"

I'm 100% guilty of this. In fact, it might be my process. If someone has an idea that is out of my comfort zone, I immediately say "No." Then, I start to think about it. Is it really such a bad idea? What is so bad about it? Why do I hate this idea? Ok, I really don't hate this idea. Could I change anything about it to make it a good idea? Ok, maybe it's not such a bad idea. In fact, it's kind of a great idea—with these changes. Ok. Let's do it.

Why do I jump straight to "No"? I think there are three phases of a business. When you first start your business, you're in the "Yes Phase." You say "Yes" to everything because you either don't know any better or you're afraid to say "No" and offend people. Eventually you get burned from saying "Yes" all the time and you move solidly into the "No Phase." The "No Phase" means that people ask you things and you don't even think about it, you say "No" TO EVERYTHING. And you don't care about offending any-one. And it's awesome. But after a while, you start to think, maybe some of these asks might actually be good for my business—now you're in the "Maybe Phase." You hesitate to say "No" right away. But you sure don't say "Yes." In the "Maybe Phase" you evaluate each ask and scrutinize everything to ensure it makes sense for your business.

You can't skip phases or rush them. Still in the "Yes Phase" and miserable? Don't worry, eventually you'll move over to the "No Phase" and start enjoying life again. I had been dipping my toes in the "Maybe Phase" for a while, but then I hired a great team and I cannonballed in. When you have a team that is taking care of things for you and your business, you suddenly have the luxury of time and time allows you to think ideas and opportunities through.

We don't calculate the cost of doing nothing

This is probably the most over-looked aspect of risk-avoidance. There is an actual cost (in $) for not taking risks in your business. Sure, it's risky to hire employees—but if you do nothing what will that inaction cost you?

Let's look at my earlier example of sustained injury due to leaf-raking. If I had hired someone to teach 2 of my 4 classes and I paid them $20/class, I would have been out $40/day plus any employer-paid taxes. But, that would have given me an extra 2 hours each day. If I used those extra 2 hours to work on a marketing plan to bring in some new clients, I could easily pay for that teacher and then some. If during my extra 2 hours, I was able to attract just 1 new client who purchased our $99 Intro Month, which is one month of unlimited class, I just covered the cost of that teacher plus an additional $59. Or did I?

Remember the power of the referral. What if that 1 client referred 3 friends who all purchased the $99 Intro Month? What if they all bought socks and tank tops and leggings because we had cute clothes for sale? And then, what if those friends told some of their friends and they bought classes? Do you see how the value of hiring an additional teacher meant an increase in thousands of dollars to the studio? Those referrals would have potentially added thousands of dollars to our monthly revenues. And they were all the result of hiring an employee to give me additional time to work ON my business.

If you're hesitant to take a risk and hire employees to scale your fitness studio, it's important to ask yourself: "What am I losing by my inaction?" There is a cost for doing nothing. If you don't act, your competition will.

So, let's dive into how to make great hiring decisions so your business can keep growing.

How to stay on your toes:

In this chapter, I discussed what I like to call, the Employee Risk Myth. In other words, scaling your business won't be risky if you assess the risk and develop a plan to mitigate that risk.

1. *What is your definition of risk?*

2. *Have you avoided hiring enough employees out of fear?*

3. *What do you think the cost for your inaction is (in $)?*

CHAPTER 6

How to Hire a Rock Star Team

Where are all the good employees? Is there an echo in the room?

But seriously, when I talk to small business owners or even friends that work for large corporations if the subject of hiring comes up the following is said:

> "It's so hard to find good people."
> "I can never find anyone good to work for me."
> "I wish I didn't have employees."

Are you depressed yet? I mean, how are you supposed to grow a business that works without you so you can be the leader of your fitness community if you have to rely on hiring employees that apparently aren't good enough? Or possibly don't exist?

But before you throw in the towel, let's consider two things:

1. If you think you're never going to find these "good people" you won't. END OF STORY. Stop the negative thoughts.

2. If you are having trouble finding these "good people" perhaps you're not attracting the RIGHT people.

And that is what I'd like to focus on in this discussion—finding the RIGHT people for your business. Awesome. Tell me how to run a killer ad and where to place it to find these perfect employees. Not so fast…

First, as the owner of your business, you need to do a little bit of work before running ads, interviewing, etc. You need to define your business goals to attract the right candidates. If you don't define your business, your employees will do it for you and that's not ideal since you're the one with the vision of where the business will go and you're taking all the risk to get there. What you'll want to do is sit down and write out your business Vision, Mission and Culture Statements.

The Vision Statement

The Vision Statement will tell anyone reading what the business objective is. It should be short, sweet and to the point. Below is my studios' Vision Statement to get you started:

Pure Barre Winston-Salem & Pure Barre Clemmons' Vision Statement:

Dedicated to achieving strength, confidence and smiles.

Some additional background … We want all of our clients to become stronger and more confident by taking Pure Barre classes. We also want our clients to have fun and look forward to their time in the studio. Notice that this Vision is extremely broad and something we'll never really master—we'll be continuously working towards this goal as long as the studios are open.

The Mission Statement

The Mission Statement defines what the business does and goes into a little more detail than the Vision Statement. It might delve into how you will accomplish the ideas established in the Vision Statement. The Mission Statement should also serve as a guide to your employees of how they might conduct themselves in your business. Here is what I came up with for my studios:

Pure Barre Winston-Salem & Pure Barre Clemmons Mission Statement:

Pure Barre Winston-Salem and Pure Barre Clemmons is a team of committed, motivated and focused people who are always striving to be strong, balanced and caring. We will work to ensure that everyone who walks through our doors is treated like family and leaves with a smile on their face. We will challenge our clients to learn their true strength while achieving their fitness goals. We believe that working out should be fun and that Pure Barre helps us live a balanced life which allows us to be our best selves.

The Culture Statement

And finally, the Culture Statement or the core values of your business—what you and your team value. This is what you want to spend some time putting together. If you don't define your business culture, your employees will, and they might have other ideas than you—like, bad ideas. And the whole point is to get you the best employees that fit into YOUR unique business culture. You're in charge so you get to establish the rules.

When I put my studios' Culture Statement together, I already had a team of about 15 working for me so I used the creation of our Culture Statement as a team-building exercise. Having your team help you develop the Culture Statement allows them to be involved with these significant changes to your business and also give them "buy-in" to this new declaration of what your company values and is all about. If someone does not share your values, you'll find out pretty quickly because they'll leave. But, you'll be able to replace them with someone who does share what's important to you and the rest of your team.

I knew I wanted to define the areas of values, passion, excellence/high performance, communication, development & continuous learning and taking class. I asked the team to write out short descriptions of what they thought about these areas in relation to our team.

It was great! They all put a lot of effort into it and came up with some great ideas that I would never have thought of. I combined these thoughts as well as my own (I am the owner after all) and now we have a Culture Statement that you can read below:

Pure Barre Winston-Salem & Pure Barre Clemmons Culture:

Values: We believe in living a healthy, balanced lifestyle and support the journey our clients take as they do the same. We greet each client by name or with a smile to show them that they are valued from the second they enter the door. We build connections with our clients through fitness, strength and a supportive Pure Barre community.

Passion: We work together as a team to make our clients love to come to Pure Barre class and hate to leave the studio. We want to help everyone who walks through our studio doors to perform and achieve things they previously thought impossible. We truly love what we do and tell everyone how great Pure Barre is and how it has transformed our bodies. If we meet someone who has never tried a Pure Barre class, we want them to be as passionate and devoted to the technique as we are. Pure Barre is bigger than just going through the motions.

Excellence/High Performance: We have high expectations for ourselves and we encourage each other and our clients to strive for excellence in each and every class. We set the standard to make each class better than the one that preceded it—whether we're teaching or taking.

Communication: We work to ensure that no client leaves the studio feeling confused or unsatisfied. During class, we strive for clear cues and inspiring words. There is genuine communication that takes place between clients and Team members to strengthen our Pure Barre community and complement the physical work that's taking place in the studio.

Development & Continuous Learning: We constantly challenge ourselves to learn, improve and build on our skills. We believe that you can always learn something from each of our Team members no matter their level of experience.

Taking Class: We love Pure Barre and can't imagine a life without taking class each week. When we take class, we are a positive example to each other and our clients. Pure Barre is "your hour to change your body" and we make it a priority.

So, if you own a franchise, do you still have to create your Vision, Mission, and Culture statements? Yes you do! Owning a franchise is great because you essentially purchase a working operating system. You don't have to develop anything brand new. The product is already created. The sales strategy is already planned. You just have to execute it.

Unfortunately, this operating system does not include your own unique company culture. Even if your Franchisor has these things (mine didn't have all of them), it makes sense for you to expand on the Culture statement because you may place value on some additional points that will make your location excel.

If you don't define your business culture, your employees will, and they might have other ideas than you—like, bad ideas that will limit your business growth and success.

To succeed at owning a franchise beyond what the Franchisor supports, you must create your unique Company Culture—write it down and hire only employees that believe in that Culture and act according to its guidelines.

Since this book is committed to offering you practical advice you can start using right away, I've created this handy worksheet to help you start thinking about and writing statements for your own business.

Writing Your Vision, Mission and Culture Statements

You'll want to start by creating your Vision Statement, then the business' Mission Statement and finally craft the Culture Statement.

The Vision Statement
Your Vision Statement declares what your business objective is. It's helpful to ask yourself and think about the following when creating the Vision Statement:

1. What is the "why" of the business? What is the purpose of the business?
2. Are there 1-3 specific things that the business does every day that separate it from the competition?
3. How would your best clients or customers describe what your business does to fulfil their needs and keep them coming back?

Once you have some ideas written down, think about the following:

1. If you removed a word or added a word, how would that change the meaning of your Vision Statement?
2. Is there a better or more descriptive word you could use?

SHE'S ON HER TOES

3. Does your Vision Statement reflect your priorities as a business owner and separate you from other businesses competing for your clients or customers?

The Mission Statement
It's easy to get carried away and write volumes about the mission of your business. Try and keep it to one or two descriptive paragraphs. Start by expanding on your Vision Statement. Think of the Mission Statement as a guide not only for your potential clients, but also for your employees. Ask yourself the following when establishing your Mission Statement:

1. How can I take my Vision Statement and expand it to tell my clients and employees what to expect when they come into my business?
2. Who am I? Who are my employees? What makes us different? Why should potential clients come to my business?
3. What are the 1-3 things that we want to achieve for our clients? How will we make those 1-3 things happen for our clients?
4. If I put the Mission Statement in a frame, would it make sense? Would it inspire my clients to visit my business more frequently or buy more from me?

Writing Your Vision, Mission and Culture Statements

The Culture Statement

Writing and developing your Culture Statement is probably one of THE most important things you'll do as a business owner—so it's important to spend some time on it and get it right. Once you have a Culture Statement, you'll know exactly what you're looking for when hiring new employees—only people who agree with the values you've identified in your business' Culture Statement. If someone doesn't quite fit, they aren't right for your business. Don't worry about eliminating potential hires if you've had difficulty hiring in the past. Once you establish what you stand for, those are the type of people you will attract to apply for open positions going forward.

If you already have a few employees, developing the Culture Statement can be a great team exercise and allow your existing team to have "buy-in" to this new strategic change in your business. I found that creating the parameters by providing my team a list of the values to be included in the Culture Statement and then having them elaborate on what those values were or meant to them provided the best results. When creating your business Culture Statement ask yourself the following:

1. What are the 4-6 core values that I believe in and want my employees to find important? Note: You can select more, but it's important to keep things concise and manageable for your team.
2. Is there one thing that is extremely important for all of us to value? Or is there one thing that we all value right now that makes us special?

Once you've created your list of core values, share them with your team and ask for their feedback about what those values mean to them and how they would apply those values to working in your business. I gave my team a week to get their responses to me and then I read them and compiled the best ideas, along with my own into the finished product. When crafting the final Culture Statement ask yourself the following:

1. Did my employees have similar things to say about each value?
2. Did any unique ideas emerge?
3. Should any of the values be revised based on their responses?
4. Do any of my ideas conflict with the responses given by my employees?
5. How can we use these values to improve our customer service and strengthen how we work together as a team?
6. Will anyone on my team not agree with these values? How will I handle that and approach that employee?

Once you have final versions of your Vision, Mission and Culture Statements, you'll want to consider putting each on display for both your clients and team to see and be reminded of on a regular basis. If you have an employee handbook or operations manual, all three should be included for easy reference. As your business grows, you'll want to review all three statements to ensure they still reflect the priorities of your business. I like to review at the beginning of each year along with any overall strategy changes I'm considering.

Create a Job Description

Ok. So now you have your business Vision, Mission and Culture Statements and you're feeling pretty good. Ready for that ad? Not quite yet. You'll also want to create a job description of the position you're wanting to fill. What do you want this new employee to do on a day-to-day basis? Do they need special skills to fulfill the duties of the job? Write it all out and get as organized as possible so when you meet with your candidates for interviews you already know what this new employee will need to do and what personality traits or skills they'll need to have to meet your requirements.

Now you can write your ad. Yes! Finally!

Write Your Killer Ad

Here is an ad I recently used to attract over 50 applicants to work in a front desk associate position at my studios.

Pure Barre Winston-Salem & Pure Barre Clemmons Front Desk Associate Ad

If you're the front desk associate we're looking for… You'll be…

Friendly, charming, enthusiastic and conscientious … You'd have a passion for Pure Barre, have high standards and be described as courteous, mature and a team player…

You'll be responsible for 3 major roles with Pure Barre Winston-Salem/Pure Barre Clemmons—greeting clients and checking them into class, selling athletic clothing and accessories and daily operations, including keeping the studio clean and inviting as well as working with our teachers to provide a superior experience to our clients.

You'll need to be well presented, trustworthy, punctual and love smiling. If you aren't already taking Pure Barre classes, you'll need to commit to taking 3-4 classes each week—as loving Pure Barre and taking class is a key element of our culture. You'll be eager to take this opportunity to learn, grow and achieve well above average results. You'll apply the skills you already have in sales, windows-based programs and have worked previously in a similar role.

If you believe this is you, be ready to show us why when you call to leave the answers to the following 3 questions:

1. When was the last time you did something nice for someone "just because"?

    Explain why.

2. What is the best word that describes you? Please pick only one.

3. What was the last book you read?

I placed this ad on our studios' Facebook and Instagram pages as well as through Hiringsteps.com, which reaches out to a number of job positing sites. I highly recommend using Hiringsteps.com for its ease of use as well as the great features the software offers to screen your applicants. Hiringsteps.com is a monthly subscription that can be cancelled at any time. So, you can keep it going if you are going to be hiring multiple employees over a period of time, or cancel after finding someone during a one-month period. In addition, Hiringsteps.com has integrated the call-in feature for your applicants to leave their messages.

I actually met several sales representatives from Hiringsteps.com at a conference and they thanked me for sharing how great the service is in a previous blog post on www.shesonhertoes.com. As it turns out, many who read it, called to set up accounts. I don't get any incentives by referring Hiringsteps.com, it's just a great service that can give you a serious advantage when trying to hire employees and grow your team.

If you decided you didn't want to use Hiringsteps.com, you could always set up a Google Voice account to keep your applicant messages saved along with transcripts.

You've probably never seen an ad like this, am I right? My business coach, Mary Ann, gave me this template and recommended having every applicant call to answer those 3 questions. Why?

For two reasons:

1. **It self-selects the best candidates.** I had over 50 people send their resume for this position, but only 30 left messages on our account number that recorded all the calls and also provided me a transcript of each call to print out and keep with each applicant's resume. Boom! Already found the best 30 people in the group because they can follow directions.

2. **This position requires the candidate to be friendly and have a great phone presence.** By asking candidates to leave a message, I already know how these applicants will sound on the phone to clients. Since a few of them rambled on and didn't have the best phone presence, I was able to narrow down to about 20 applicants.

Setting up the Interviews

Now interviewing 20 people would take forever and I don't have that kind of time. In fact, I really only had two hours to get these interviews done. What to do?!

Two words: Group interview. Group interviews are great because they save you time and you can see how the candidates react to each other. Are they too aggressive? Are they rude? Did one cut another off to get more talking time in? Did one just say the same things as the others without coming up with original answers? All great things to learn as you're building your team.

Next, I sent each candidate an email inviting them to a group interview during a time that worked for me. Some couldn't make it and we actually had to set up two separate interview times because I wanted to meet with a few select candidates that couldn't make the initial time I had set up. Boom! 10 people ready to interview on two different days. Things are getting a little more manageable.

Before the interviews, I ranked each candidate from 1 to 10. One being the most qualified and ten being the least. At this point all ten were qualified, but it's important to be organized and make sure you are creating an interview process that gets you the best of the best. I also had my Mission, Vision and Culture Statements ready as well as a few questions that I wanted to make sure were answered by each candidate.

During the interviews, Mary Ann did most of the questioning so I could listen and take notes, which was extremely helpful. I'm sure many of you have interviewed someone and you're so focused on what the next question is and what's coming up next that you don't really listen to the answers the candidate is giving. You could have another employee or friend help you if you don't have a business coach. But ... maybe you should get a business coach.

Mary Ann introduced me and gave a brief description of the business and the role. She then had me read our Vision, Mission and Culture Statements (Yes! All the work putting those ideas together finally paid off!). You might want to talk about what it's like to work at your business, review the position description (Remember, you wrote that out already), pay structure, whatever is important to let the candidates know. At this point, Mary Ann says "If any of this doesn't sound good, you are welcome to leave. We totally understand that this might not be the position for you."

No one left because, of course, my business is amazing and working for me would be your dream come true—ok, just kidding. But no one left. If they did, that would be totally fine. It would ensure that I was only selecting the best people that WANT TO WORK FOR ME. Another self-selection point reached.

Then the candidates are asked individual questions and have time to ask their own questions. And if I have any more questions for each of them, I'll ask at that time including availability, when they could potentially start, or elaborating on a previous statement—those kinds of things. As the last step of the interview, the candidates are asked to fill out a questionnaire which is a great way to get any final thoughts. The questionnaire had the following questions:

Pure Barre Winston-Salem & Pure Barre Clemmons Front Desk Associate Final Interview Questions

1. What did you hear that impressed or touched you?

2. What have you done in the past that you believe you could add value to the story I've told you?

3. What one hurdle, what impossible hurdle have you had to overcome in your life that has caused you to believe that you're a keeper?

4. What is it about the position we described that appeals to you?

5. Any other comments?

6. After everything you've seen and heard do you want to go further in this interview process?

You probably want to give everyone about ten or fifteen minutes to write their responses. I had one candidate write some very personal and touching things on her questionnaire. I'm so glad we had this last step because it made me understand more about her and she established herself as a person I wanted to hire. And now she works for me and is a great asset to the Team.

Sweet! Interviews are over. You can now compare the responses you got with the ranking you made before the interviews commenced and select your top choices.

Wouldn't this process have been nice to learn in business school?! I mean, it would be so great to learn some practical ways to actually hire great people instead of hearing the "you're only as strong as your team" lecture. Sigh.

You've identified a great new employee called them. Hired them. Everything is awesome, right? Wrong. This is just the beginning. You now have to develop this employee, make sure they are working to their potential and most importantly make sure they are working to add value your business.

Oh man. This business ownership thing just got real.

How to stay on your toes:

In this chapter, I revealed the steps I took to create my business' Vision, Mission and Culture Statements. I also explained step-by-step how I placed an employment ad and interviewed multiple candidates to fill any position at my studios.

1. *Do you have a Vision, Mission and Culture Statement for your business?*
2. *Do you have an identified hiring process that's written down?*
3. *Do you have job descriptions for all the positions in your business?*

CHAPTER 7

How to Lead Those Rock Stars to Success

For me, the words "team" and "building" conjure up bad memories from business school. I start thinking back to trust falls or building tricycles and racing them as full-grown adults. I still shutter at thoughts of putting together a boat made out of nothing but a piece of cardboard and some plastic wrap to "sail" across a small pond in my business clothes—yeah, you get f**king soaked and have to drive home thinking: "What in the world did that teach me about working together as a team? We had to build a boat out of cardboard that doesn't float and I basically went for an unexpected swim." Not that I'm still bitter about these experiences ...

I think there is a misunderstanding about what teambuilding really is for a small business. Teambuilding is any activity that enhances the work your team will complete at your business. Activities like reviewing your specific operations processes, learning about a new product or service, and sales training would all be considered teambuilding. Activities like getting dinner together or going out for drinks are not teambuilding exercises and in my opinion, should be considered rewards for meeting business goals.

Now that you've spent a lot of time and effort hiring the best possible team, you've got to spend time developing and training them. There's nothing worse in life than wasted talent and trust me your team has talent, so use it!

"But it's so hard to delegate," you might say. "I can do everything myself faster and better than my employees." Um, remember what we talked about? If you don't grow your business, then it's dying. And, what's the definition of a fitness business, again? Oh yeah, a profitable enterprise that works without you so you can be the leader in your fitness community ... find the time to document all of your business processes so your employees have a reference to refer to on how to do everything that you do. You might find that someone on your team does things better than you. Wouldn't that be great!

Maybe you write an operations manual. Maybe you write out sales sheets. Maybe you write out role-playing scenarios to teach your team how to combat opposition to a sale of your product or service. Maybe you write out phone scripts. Whatever you do, write it down and teach your employees how to do it like you would. For the record, I do all of those things at my studios. Well, actually I have my amazing manager create them. I review, and then she teaches everyone. Delegating. It works when you have the RIGHT team working for you.

To help you start documenting all the processes in your business, I've created this handy worksheet.

Start Documenting Your Business Processes & Create an Operations Manual

Creating an Operations Manual for your business seems like a huge time commitment and maybe even a waste of time ... until you're away from your business and your employees need you to help them complete a task that could have easily been accomplished if you had just written it down. Ah!

If it seems too daunting to create an entire manual for your team, break it down into smaller parts and just keep adding to it. Or start with the parts that you must complete and assign other sections to an employee for your review. When documenting your business processes ask yourself the following:

1. What are the most important processes or activities that happen in my business on a daily basis?
2. What processes or activities will I eventually need to delegate to my employees?
3. Do I need to keep detailed instructions about our systems including alarm, electrical panel, or equipment maintenance on hand so everything is maintained properly at the business?
4. If I was ever out of town or if my employees couldn't reach me, what instructions would they need to keep the business running?

Once you've determined your most important processes and what information your employees will need at-once to keep your business running if you weren't there, ask yourself the following to start writing:

1. What are the step-by-step actions that I need to write out to complete the task or process?

2. What special instructions or information do I use to complete a task that my employees don't have access to right now?
3. Must the task be completed exactly as written, or is there some room for an employee to make changes?
4. Are my directions clear and concise? Would everyone reading understand the objective?

After you've written out the process, it's a good idea to have your employees review each of the steps to ensure you haven't left anything out or have made anything unclear. Finally, you'll need to determine where to keep your operations manual so everyone can access it or whether you'll want to give copies to each individual employee.

Then after my team and I meet a sales goal, the team is rewarded. During one of our most fun evenings out, we all went and got pedicures. After all, it's tough staying on your toes!

But wait, you skipped a step. You might be thinking, "How do I motivate my team to work hard and focus on activities that benefit my business?" Sure, they work for me, but what now? Below are the five most compelling ways that I've found to motivate my team:

1. Don't micromanage

Otherwise known as "empowering" your team, if you want to keep things positive. I talk a lot about empowering my team during our team meetings (we meet once a month, although you might want to meet with your team more often). To me, this means it's ok to make mistakes. Or maybe you do something a little different then I would and as long as the task is completed within any given parameters, that's ok. Mistakes are "ok" as long as you learn from them and don't repeat them. I know I've empowered everyone when there aren't any sticky notes on the computer when I come into the studio.

You know what I mean ... you walk in and instead of starting to work on YOUR list of priorities, you have like 80 sticky notes all over the computer and desk because someone didn't know how to take care of something. I hate sticky notes. And I've actually wondered if I stopped buying them, would my team have to take care of everything on their own because they couldn't leave a note for the next person?!

For the record, the sticky notes have almost stopped. Yea team! Stay strong!

2. Communicate your vision and sales goals with everyone

I used to be a little secretive with my business financials with my team. How dumb was that?! If I don't tell my team what it is we're trying to accomplish or what is driving our two studios' sales each month, how will they know what to work on? Now, at our team meetings I review our previous month's sales and talk about what drove the numbers to the level we achieved (ie. Class sales in Clemmons increased compared to last month because we saw an increase in $99 Intro Month purchases with our Bring Your Friends promotion. Or...Clothing sales in Reynolda Village increased because we had some really cute things and focused on upselling tanks if someone purchased a pair of leggings— we sold 30 more tanks than last month). I think I used to keep our sales information close to the vest because I didn't trust a few members of my team. Now that I've spent a great deal of time outlining our Vision, Mission and Culture statements, I know that my current team is committed to our success and 100% invested. I've learned the more information I share, the better our performance. As a bonus, my team can actually review evidence that their hard work is paying off.

3. Push their limits

You never really know what your team is capable of until you push them to work their hardest or most efficiently. This can backfire, however, if you have unrealistic expectations and are disappointed by what you perceive as lackluster results. I have found that in order to set my team up for success with a tough sales goal, it's best that they work together. Meaning the entire team has to be rewarded for meeting the goal, not just the top salesperson.

4. Develop leadership within the organization

Eventually your business will reach a level where you won't be able to do everything yourself. So ... you have to make sure someone else has the leadership to help you out and run the place. This can be tricky because some people who have authority positions aren't well-respected. As we discussed before, anyone who doesn't quite fit in at your business is missing a key element of your Culture and should never be given a leadership role unless you're prepared for them to fail miserably.

I only know one way to develop leadership in my team and that's through leading by example. I have an amazing manager. Of course, she was probably perfect before she started working for me, but I'd like to think that she picked up a few things from me including being prepared, decisive thinking, not being afraid to make changes if something's not working and giving everyone the freedom to operate (ie. no micromanaging).

5. Celebrate your success

It's so easy as business owners to be down on ourselves for not doing something or not meeting a goal. And what happens when you finally do something amazing? What do you say? "Well, it's about time." This is so bad.

You need to take the time to celebrate your and your team's success. The easiest way to do this is to give your team a goal and tell them the reward to motivate them. Now you can't not celebrate if they reach the goal because you've already put the reward out there. And no one likes a "take back."

There you have it. 5 of the most compelling ways I've found to motivate my team—hopefully a few if not all work for you. But really it all boils down to trusting your team to do their best—which goes back to avoiding micromanaging!

Remember, when your team is working FOR your business, you are free to work ON your business. You will have time to develop a killer marketing strategy, or complete less glamorous tasks like reconciling your bank and credit card statements and paying the rent. It is imperative, however, that the team is always learning. That means, you are always challenging them, giving them new goals and spending time supporting their efforts.

Uh, it never ends, does it? Nope. But, if owning and operating a fitness business was easy, everyone would do it! Besides there is nothing better than rewarding your team for a job well done. When I took my team out for those pedicures mentioned earlier, seeing them all smiling and happy was sweet. Ok, maybe they were just buzzed from drinking wine. Don't ruin it for me! In my mind, they were happy to celebrate working hard and meeting our goal of bringing in new clients during the previous sales month. It was a tough goal. Almost unrealistic. But they did it! What did I say about talent?

How to stay on your toes:

In this chapter, I discussed what activities fall under the definition of teambuilding and what do not. I also provided the best 5 ways I've found to motivate my team to work their hardest and smartest.

1. *What teambuilding have you organized for your employees? How often?*
2. *Do you find it difficult to delegate to your employees?*
3. *Which of the 5 ways to motivate your team will work for your business?*

Part 3: How to Develop Your Own Business & Leadership Skills

"There are two ways of spreading light: to be the candle or the mirror that reflects it."
—EDITH WHARTON, NOVELIST

"If your actions create a legacy that inspires others to dream more, learn more, do more and become more, then, you are an excellent leader."
—DOLLY PARTON, SINGER-SONGWRITER, ACTRESS AND BUSINESSWOMAN

CHAPTER 8

How to Succeed at Owning a Fitness Franchise Beyond What the Franchisor Supports

In the past five years, boutique fitness franchises have become more abundant investment opportunities. Brands specializing in yoga, barre, circuit & interval training, and cycling have all increased their locations and class offerings looking to capitalize on consumer behaviors that include spending less time going to big-box, generic gyms, yet still placing overall health as a priority. The industry will only get bigger and more competitive as the so-called mega-trend of health-conscious living develops further and capital from individual investors or private equity companies is injected into top brands.

Health-minded individuals will have more choices of where to spend their fitness dollar and as a result, they'll demand more from your business to keep their patronage. While increased competition can be scary, established fitness business owners who have worked to create a strong community, can view increased competition as an opportunity—a welcomed opportunity to let new competitors who are less-capable and less-seasoned highlight what actually makes your fitness community so great.

That's right. If you've put in the work to build your team so that you can work on your business and become a leader in your studio's health and fitness community, any competitor shortcomings will only showcase how great your studio truly is.

The ideas discussed in this chapter are directed towards fitness franchisees, however, these concepts easily apply to any independent-owned boutique fitness studio as well. Business is business, after all.

Statistically, franchised businesses are able to bring in greater revenues than independently-owned businesses. The U.S. Small Business Administration has found that on average, a franchise can earn five times the first-year revenue of the average independent business and over 95% of franchises that open are still successfully in business five years later.

Since franchisees typically get more training and have more resources than independents, this makes sense. In addition, the business concept of the franchise has been tested and proven. So why, if you own a franchise, does it seem so hard? Why do franchise owners struggle? Why does it seem like at times you can never get ahead operating your franchise?

If you have a passion for fitness, buying a fitness franchise can be a great way to quickly ramp up a business. You don't have to reinvent the wheel or even invent one. That's already been done for you. You're buying a proven concept that also includes a corporate team to help you find the ideal location, help you establish a business plan, and in many cases, help you market to your future clients.

But there are some pitfalls to owning a franchise as well. For instance, the New York City fitness market is vastly different than Chicago or Boston and all are completely different from Winston-Salem, NC. What works well in a big city might not work at all in your city or community.

By owning a franchise, you inherently give up some control in operating your business. If the franchisor rolls out a national campaign promoting a particular class package or sales funnel, you have to participate, whether it is problematic for your clients or not.

Nevertheless, fitness franchises continue to grow at a rapid pace, so it's hard to discount the business model.

As previously discussed, I own and operate two Pure Barre franchises and both are successful. That is, both are profitable and will run without me there. I can be out networking, working on my businesses, sleeping, or on vacation and know that classes are being taught and purchases rung up. Don't get me wrong, I work really hard—but so does my Team.

Owning a Pure Barre franchise is great. The franchisor gives me support that I would not otherwise have if I just owned my own barre or fitness studio. And I do have some independence while making marketing decisions that best fit my location and client needs. If I don't like something, I can call or email and express my unhappiness—if it can be fixed right away, it is. Bigger changes might not happen immediately, but at least I'm being listened to.

It is important to remember, however, that the interests of the franchisee and the interests of the franchisor are often at odds, which starts us off on how to succeed at owning a franchise beyond what the franchisor supports …

The number one concern of the franchisor is revenue growth. As long as your franchise continues to grow revenue, the franchisor is happy. See, the franchisor collects a monthly royalty and as long as that monthly payment keeps getting bigger, all is good. The problem with that is as a franchisee, your primary concern is your net income growth—or profit. If your profit is growing you're happy. As a franchisee, if you could gain more profit by lowering expenses and not increasing revenue or even decreasing revenue, that's awesome. Good work! Unfortunately, the franchisor doesn't see it that way.

This juxtaposition of interests does not make franchise ownership bad and it doesn't mean doom for your business. It is just extremely important that you understand these conflicting interests—the better you understand this, the more successful you'll be. If you're looking at your monthly reports from the franchisor and think you're killing it because your top line is growing—what are your own financials telling you about your net income growth?

If you aren't making any money (negative net income) or just scraping by to pay your bills—that's not awesome. IF YOU'RE NOT PAYING YOURSELF—YOU NEED TO BE. I know a lot of franchise owners that don't pay themselves regularly but talk about how their business is doing well. Hummm … really?

Does not paying yourself seem like it would fit into the definition of a fitness business. No, it does not. The work you put into your business has a monetary value and should be given back to you each month. Not able to pay yourself what you're worth? Start by looking at all your monthly expenses and carefully justifying each one.

I evaluate my business expenses at the end of each month. Sometimes it's obvious that a line-item can be cut going forward, other times, it's more difficult to evaluate the importance of spending. As a business owner, the important thing to ask yourself when evaluating expenses is this: "Could I use this money more effectively to enhance my clients and our fitness community if I spent it somewhere else?" Since money is a finite resource—meaning you don't have a limitless supply—it's always a good idea to make sure it's being used in the most effective way. One area where money seems to just get sucked out of our bank accounts and thus lowering our net income, is marketing.

What is Marketing?

There seems to be a lot of mystery surrounding marketing in boutique fitness and yet, it's probably one of your studio's largest dollar spends each month after payroll, rent and franchise royalties (if you own a franchise). Specifically, fitness owners want to know what works and what doesn't. And how the heck do you KNOW if your marketing is working?!

There was a time when marketing, admittedly was the part of my business that I would have rather spent as little time as possible. The reason being that it seemed like I was spending money marketing my studios and then I never really knew if it was working. I knew marketing, specifically paid advertising, was important to attract new clients, but I never really felt confident about where to spend my marketing budget. Was my message reaching my ideal client? Did that person feel compelled to come into the studios to take class? Who knows?! I was approaching marketing in the wrong way.

The American Marketing Association has come up with the following definition of marketing.

Definition of Marketing

Marketing is the activity, set of institutions, and processes for creating, communicating, delivering and exchanging offerings that have value for customers, clients, partners, and society at large. https://www.ama.org/AboutAMA/Pages/Definition-of-Marketing.aspx

Sweet. I just reread that definition three times and I'm still not sure what it's supposed to mean. For small businesses, marketing is the cost of acquiring customers. And it wasn't until I embraced this definition of marketing that I actually got good at it.

Maybe you're a marketing wiz, but for me, thinking of marketing as the cost of acquiring a customer or simply, what makes sense for me to spend to acquire a customer, was mind blowing. Marketing was always kind of a nuisance and I was never sure how much to spend. But this actually made sense.

So basically, you need to figure out the lifetime value of your ideal customer. Ask yourself: "How much revenue will I get from this customer from an initial purchase, over a year, over several years?" Once you have that value as a dollar amount, you'll be able to determine what makes sense to acquire that customer. If your customer may only make one purchase, then you'll likely want to spend a lesser percentage of the revenue they generate to get them to buy. If your customer is making predictable or reoccurring purchases and there is a high likelihood that you can upsell them on other products and services that you offer, then you can spend more. I've created this worksheet to get you started:

Calculate the Lifetime Value of Your Average Customer

You likely already have all the information needed to determine the Lifetime Value of your Average Customer. I also like to know the Lifetime Value of my top clients too. Knowing these numbers gives you a starting point to determine your marketing budget, but it's also a great motivator for your team. Instead of just losing the sale of one package or one month of classes, the studio is losing much more. Here's why:

First, let's look at the value of an average client in your business last year. To calculate this, take annual sales divided by the number of active members at your studio. For instance, if you had $500,000 in annual sales and 500 active clients, they would have an average value of $1,000 that year.

$$\$500,000 / 500 = \$1,000$$

Next, you'll want to determine the Lifetime Value of your top clients. If you use MindBody, which is the client management software we use at my studios, you can run a "Big Spenders" report to determine the value of your top clients during the previous year. From the report, simply complete the same calculation using the total revenue earned from these top clients divided by your top 10 or 20 top clients.

But this is just the value of your average and top clients over one year. You'll need to determine how long your typical client stays with your business. This number can be a little tricky to determine, but I did the best I could looking at my top 20 clients and how long they'd been taking class. Then I did a simple average to come up with 3 years. Assuming you have a similar number, the Lifetime Value of the average client in this example would be $3,000.

Or is it? You likely receive referrals from each client that frequents your business. You'll want to determine the average referrals received. Let's pretend you just get 1 referral from each client—you probably get more—but this is an example meant to illustrate a concept. Your Lifetime Value of an average client would be $6,000+!

Instead of losing the value of one class package or one month of class, failure to retain a client could mean the loss of thousands to your business. Yikes! Another reason to make sure you have a great team in place.

If you've been struggling with marketing and attracting new clients to your business, then changing your perspective on what marketing is can have a profound impact on your business growth. And for franchisees, can make an even bigger difference in your bottom line, or your profit. The more effectively you spend your marketing budget, the lower your cost to acquire clients will be and ultimately, the better off your business will be.

Only you are keeping tabs on your expenses and working to control costs while growing the business. Generally speaking, the more profit you can make from your business, the happier you are as the owner.

Ok. Great. But HOW do I successfully market my fitness studio? Isn't that what this book is all about, teaching practical things that I can start doing now? You bet it is! Let me share with you my strategy for generating a steady stream of leads to my studios including how to test and measure the ads so you know they're working.

Lead Generation

When I opened my first studio about 5 years ago, I chose a location that was amazingly perfect for the two groups of clients I was trying to attract. Clients literally did the marketing for me by referring friends and I was constantly seeing new faces in classes throughout the day. And the business grew. It was amazing. But this was not typical and certainly did not include any type of business plan to generate predictable, solid leads.

Fast forward to when I opened my second studio and right before it opened, I got really sick—like I couldn't leave the house because I had shingles on my face. It was not amazing and yet another example of why it's important to hire and build a solid team because owning a business shouldn't make you sick or incapacitated.

Because I was struggling to simply take care of my basic needs (thankfully I had some amazing friends who brought me meals every day), I didn't have a lot of time or energy to execute a lead-generation campaign and ... the studio did amazing. No, actually the opposite. We really struggled building our client base. I've since redeemed myself and will share how I created a way to bring in steady, predictable leads to both of my studios.

Are you skeptical? If you are, that's cool. I'm going to take a stab in the dark and say that if you are skeptical, you haven't been tracking your existing marketing campaigns. Am I correct? It's ok. But, you need to start tracking.

First Things First, Start Tracking Your Marketing Campaigns

Before we jump into things, it's important to discuss the concept of tracking your marketing campaigns. First, ask yourself: Where do I get my clients from? Newspaper or magazine ads, Facebook, Instagram, ads on Facebook and Instagram, referrals, walk-ins? Make a list and try to give a percentage to each source.

Second, ask yourself: Am I currently paying money to advertise and I haven't received any clients from that campaign? If the answer is yes, then stop spending that money. Cancel the ad or whatever it is. It's not working. If you're not sure if you are gaining leads from a campaign, start tracking and see what you find out. As we've already discussed, money is finite, and you want to use it in the most effective way possible to help you build your fitness community.

I used to have an advertisement in a local monthly magazine. At first, it was great and probably brought in close to 30 new clients over the course of two months (not too shabby), but after a while, it didn't work and nobody mentioned that's where they had heard about us. So, I don't run that ad anymore. Start tracking your marketing campaigns and see what you find out. If something isn't working like you thought, it's ok to cancel and move on.

Find Out What Does Work to Reach New Clients

Now that you have eliminated any marketing campaigns that aren't working for you, you've freed up some money to redirect towards the things that do actually work to drive new leads to your business. Now ask yourself: What's working to bring new clients to my business? Should I do more of that? Or should I investigate something new?

I have discovered that there are really only 2 marketing initiatives that work to bring new clients to my studios: client referrals and Facebook and Instagram ads. Client referrals are great because you're pretty much acquiring a lead for free and that lead almost always (like 90-95% of the time) buys our introductory offer, which is the $99 Intro Month. That's like tastes great and less filling! It's a no brainer—keep those client referrals coming all day long.

So how do you encourage client referrals? Below are all the ways that my studios encourage clients to bring their friends and family in to take class.

1. **Referral Fees:** Offer a small amount of money for existing clients who bring in friends. We offer $10 in store credit to any client who brings in a friend who purchases the $99 Intro Month. If you could acquire a new client for $10, or 10% of what they just spent, would you? Sure. That's a pretty reasonable Cost to Acquire a Customer (CAC). As a bonus, your existing clients get a benefit, they feel valued and rewarded and will be motivated to bring more of their friends to your studio.

2. **Free Class to Client Friends:** Offer a free class to the client's friends. A friend of an existing client with a membership is a qualified lead. This friend has heard how great class is, how great the studio is, how clean it is, how friendly everyone is, how great the workout is and most importantly has seen how great their friend looks now that she's been taking class. Offering them a free class simply provides no excuse for them not to come to the studio and then purchase the introductory offer because they already understand the value of the service provided. The CAC here is essentially $0. You've already

scheduled the class and the other existing clients taking that class are covering the cost of the teacher, electricity, music etc. It doesn't cost you anything to offer this free class to a client's friend.

3. **Sell Gift Cards:** Offer gift cards to encourage gifting your service. This is pretty simple. Clients can buy their friends a gift card and introduce them to the studio. Again, CAC is $0 or the nominal fee for each plastic or paper gift card/certificate.

4. **Sell Friend-Centered Promotions:** Offer a promotion to encourage clients to purchase for their friends or the friends to purchase for themselves. Again, pretty simple. At key times during the year—think Holiday, or Summer, when it's a little slower—we offer a special promotion designed to bring client friends into the studio to try class. If you spent any money advertising this promotion your CAC would be the ad spend divided by number of people purchasing—or if you just emailed your list CAC would be $0. So again, CAC is likely pretty low.

5. **Outdoor Community Class or Pop-Up Class:** Offer a free community class at an outdoor location—like a great local park, winery, brewery—any place that is easily accessible encourages your clients to gather and hang out after the class. This is a higher profile way to get attention for your studio and thus also has a higher cost including the amount of time spent organizing all the logistics of hosting a great event. You'll want to consider renting or purchasing sound equipment including a mic and speakers, marketing materials including fliers, posters, and giveaways or swag, advertising and the cost of having your team staffing the event. While the cost of hosting a community event is significantly greater than our other mentioned promotions, hosting a big event is a great way for your existing clients to bring several of their friends to try your class and can bring in dozens of

new clients at once. You'll want to calculate the CAC and carefully track new clients who purchased after your event. In addition, you'll also want to consider how your existing clients will benefit from a fun outdoor class. Community classes serve two functions, a draw to introduce potential new clients to your studio as well as a great way to retain existing clients and keep them engaged in your fitness community.

Awesome, right? Sure. This is all great. At most, you're spending about 10% of the purchase to acquire a new client and these leads are qualified, meaning they have a high likelihood of purchasing.

The only problem is—we're leaving out thousands if not tens of thousands of potential new clients by only focusing on client friends and referrals. What if the person has never heard of my business? How do I reach them?

Fast Lane Leads vs. Slow Lane Leads

I hope you're getting excited reading this because what lies below pretty much blew my mind when I first implemented it. And it's totally changed the way I look at marketing and spending my advertising budget.

Before I share the special sauce, we need to review 2 concepts.

1. I have no idea who said this, but I've read it in a few books and articles written by Mike Dillard and Russell Brunson— when they cited it they didn't know where it came from either. But here goes ... Nobody wants to buy a drill. They want to make a hole. So, you shouldn't advertise drills. You should advertise how to make a hole. You need to sell the end product or RESULT. Any light bulbs going on? Any hamsters spinning on that wheel? If you're in the fitness industry, this is such a critical concept, it's not even funny.

2. We also need to define the "Fast Lane" client and the "Slow Lane" client. Fast Lane leads are the ones we talked about above—friend referrals. They've heard of your business and are ready to buy. They already understand the value and will purchase immediately because they understand the result your product or service will give them. Remember, they saw their friend get stronger or look better and more fit from taking class, so they're ready to buy right away.

Slow Lane Leads are not ready to buy. In fact, they probably don't even know your business exists. If they do know you exist, they don't understand the value of your product or service. Maybe they don't care about working out, or they think walking is a better workout, or they get childcare at the YMCA—doesn't matter, they're not sold on you. But ... that doesn't mean they won't buy in the future. How could you introduce your business to those Slow Lane Leads? How could you get them to buy from you, eventually?

Using Facebook Ads to Reach Slow Lane Leads

You can use Facebook and Instagram ads to reach Fast Lane Leads, but Facebook and Instagram ads are the ideal way to reach Slow Lane Leads—at least that's what I've learned. So how do you do it? How do you create a Facebook or Instagram ad to reach Slow Lane Leads? Here's a step-by-step guide:

1. **Free Offer:** You need a free offer that will have value to Slow Lane Leads. This is not necessarily a free class—these people are unqualified (as of now) and a free class won't always work to teach them about your business. You need something that will "wow" them and make them think, "Huh, if this business is willing to give this away to me for free, what will I get when I make an actual purchase? That must be f**king amazing!" Trust me, you have something to give away already, or you can easily make something that will

"wow" these leads. Obtaining the free offer is dependent on this Slow Lane Lead giving you their email address and/or phone number. How else are you going to reach out to them after they click on your ad? This is how you are going to grow your contact list and convert these Slow Lane Leads to purchase and become clients.

2. **Facebook and/or Instagram Ad:** Next, you need to write your ad. The more simple the ad, the better. Make it clear. Choose one action and make that action clear—you want these Slow Lane Leads to click on your ad and download your free offer. Tell them to do this in clear, concise language.

3. **Targeted Audience:** Now, you must find your targeted audience. If you have a killer offer and a clear ad, but don't advertise to the right group, you won't have any clicks and you won't get any leads. Where to start? How about your existing client base? Do they have any over-arching common interests? Did you know that Facebook can create duplicate audiences? You can take your existing client base and Facebook can find people similar to that list—pretty cool. Or maybe you just target those who have liked your Facebook page and their friends (I mean, we already know friends are more apt to buy).

4. **Split Test the Ad:** You've figured out your offer, created your ad, found the audience and you're ready to go. Split testing the ad is an important step because, well, you just don't really know this audience, right? After all, they haven't bought from you and don't know much about your business. You don't know what makes them tick. You'll want to run a few different ads with different pictures or different copy. Maybe try testing the ad with different audiences and see which gets the best results. These tests should just be small buys—I did about $10 a day for 1 week. After you try a few

things, you'll start to see some patterns or success with one ad or one audience. Then you can adjust or go full throttle and increase your ad spend. I actually spent about 3 weeks split testing and learned some valuable information along the way. I tried 2 different offers, several different audiences and about 8 different ads.

What were my results after completing these 4 steps? After only running about 4 weeks, my ad had over a 40% conversion. That means 40% of all the people clicking on it submitted their email address and downloaded my free offer. That's pretty awesome and means my offer was resonating with my audience. In fact, I got a list of just over 100 names and emails that I can communicate to and try and convert to clients.

Fast forward, to a few months later, with one small tweak, I was able to get my conversion to over 50% when I ran my ads again. How did I do that? I'll never tell! Just kidding. I added some software that showed a pop-up box of the last person's name who had redeemed my offer and what time they redeemed, which humanizes the process and makes people see that others are interested too. To create interest, just show your targeted audience others are interested too.

From those leads I had approximately 25% purchase our $99 Intro Month, which is also a great conversion. You have to remember, however, that these leads are Slow Lane Leads, so many aren't going to purchase right away. In my case, we had about 20 purchase while the ads were running and then it took us another month to get 5 more purchases. You will likely have to reach out to them or email them multiple times to reach a sale. You'll need to create compelling and informative email content to educate these leads on why your business, product or service is something they should buy. It's harder to earn these Slow Lane Lead sales because you have to sell them on the RESULT of your product or service and most importantly, earn their trust. Slow Lane Leads are not quick to make decisions or give something a try unless they trust the result.

So, there you go. You now know the secret to successfully generate steady leads to your business. Below are a few resources you can check out to create your Facebook Lead Generation Campaign. I used all of them to create mine.

AdEspresso: This tool makes ad creation easy. You can also make several versions of your ads for your split testing. https://adespresso.com

Click Funnels: The video on the first page of this site is totally stupid. Don't let that fool you. This site is revolutionary. Once you understand what a sales funnel is, you'll wonder how you ever functioned without one. https://www.clickfunnels.com

Magnetic Sponsoring: How to Attract Endless New Leads and Distributors to You Automatically, Mike Dillard: This book was originally written for those in the network marketing business, but it's applicable to every business. Read it. That's all. http://amzn.to/2jgXTW2

Marketing is an area of business where it's important to track, test and measure to determine if the amount spent is having the desired yield of new clients to your studio. If you aren't seeing an appropriate return on your marketing spending, stop that campaign and focus the money elsewhere. If your budget is rock-solid and you're still struggling to pay yourself, take a look at your marketing and evaluate in detail, where that money is going and what it is doing to bring new clients into your studio.

Friend referrals and social media ads on Facebook and Instagram are easily trackable and allow you to reach your ideal client. Furthermore, Facebook and Instagram ads can help you develop a steady source of leads to your studio, so you'll never be wondering "Where are we going to find new clients this month?"

To succeed at owning a franchise beyond what the franchisor supports, you must look beyond franchisor-produced sales reports which only track revenue growth and focus on growing your net income. Even if you don't own a fitness franchise, these same principles apply. Hopefully the take-away from this chapter is that you are the only one looking out for your business's financial well-being. You can't rely on franchisor-produced reports to determine if your business is doing well. It's vitally important to evaluate your expenses including one of your most important, marketing, to ensure that those dollars are being used effectively to grow your revenues and then ultimately your profits. You'll need to look at what makes sense to spend to acquire each customer and then put that money to use reaching the appropriate audience.

You've hired a great team, learned how to motivate them, and learned some fundamentals on marketing and lead generation. Now it's time to learn how to be a leader.

How to stay on your toes:

In this chapter, I explained the importance of looking beyond revenue growth as a sign that your business is succeeding. Whether you own a franchise or not, it's all about net income growth. I also took an in-depth look at how to make sure your marketing budget helps your business increase revenue and net income.

1. *Do you track your current marketing expenditures? Should any of them be cancelled?*
2. *Do you have methods in place for Fast Lane and Slow Lane lead generation?*
3. *If you were to create a lead generation campaign, what would your free offer be?*

CHAPTER 9

Leadership Isn't Developed Overnight, So Start Now

Opening a business does not instantaneously make you a leader—damn. If only it did. As we've already discussed, your fitness studio requires that you hire a team of employees to run it, so you will need to learn how to manage and motivate them to run the business.

I probably spend a good 90% of my time trying to figure out how to keep my team motivated and how I can better support them to sell more. Does this shock you? At this point, I have hired an incredible team to help me run my studios. Since they complete the day-to-day operations, that frees me up to work on supporting them and working on activities that enhance my businesses. It's great—but getting to that point does take time and calculated effort. I've been working towards this point for over five years!

If you own and operate a franchise and the Franchisor offers leadership training or management training—sign up and take it! If nothing like that is offered, or you own an independent business, then it's on you to invest in yourself and learn how to lead and manage. But on a practical level, success breeds success, which furthers more success, so by simply adopting some of the proven habits of successful business owners, you can learn to be a better leader.

There are literally hundreds if not thousands of books about how to be your best in business. Some lay claim to a very specific set of morning rituals meant to improve your overall health, gain mental clarity, and increased focus. Others are all about saving time or eliminating distractions from your life. If you read between the lines, all these books are essentially telling you the same thing about productivity and leadership. Let me explain.

Do you remember that scene from **Something About Mary** where that hitchhiker is telling Ben Stiller about his new company that is "going to blow 8-Minute Abs right out of the water?" 7-Minute Abs! Unless, as Stiller points out, someone comes up with 6-Minute Abs. Seriously, who works out in 6 minutes? Great movie.

The larger point is, there will always be some flashy new way to try and decrease your time spent working from 40 hours, to 30 hours, to less than 10 hours each week. But as we've discussed throughout the earlier pages of this book, it's all about doing the work and implementing the fundamentals to improve your business.

In order to be a better leader, I think it boils down to the following three concepts:

1. **Do what's most important first—and what's most important is setting yourself up to have a great day.**

2. **Determine what you want and schedule your time with the intent to reach that goal.**

3. **Learn to be disciplined—it's the only difference between being great and being average.**

If you can work towards mastering these three concepts: prioritizing your time, determining what you want and working towards that goal, and then finally, the hardest—being disciplined—you will become a better leader for your team and increase your business success.

Do What's Most Important First

I am an early riser. I've always been able to just jump out of bed and get going when the alarm goes off. No snooze. No grace period. Once I'm up, I'm up. You can get so much done before the rest of the world gets up. It's truly amazing what you can accomplish when no one else is bothering you—I mean when you have total focus and some quiet.

Being able to get up early with a clear mind has definitely been an asset as the owner of two fitness studios. Our 6:00 AM classes are always busy with our most dedicated clients. Gotta be "on" to teach class that early in the morning.

But…at some point I started developing some really bad early morning habits that started to impact my business in a negative way. What was I doing that was so bad? When my alarm went off, the first thing I did was reach for my phone and check my email. Uh, that's not so bad, you might think. You're just checking your email. You'd check it when you got into work. I check my email all the time, no big deal. What's the problem with checking email when you get up?

Many of you in the service industry can probably relate to what I'm about to write. Clients wait until the evening to complain over email. They sit down and write out their complaints or sometimes just questions, but mostly complaints, in the evening. Since I try not to check my email past 9:00 PM, I get all these messages first thing in the morning. The first thing I see in the morning by checking my email are complaints. And while I love my clients and work really hard to make sure they are getting superior customer service, reading about all the things you and your employees are doing wrong, incorrectly or inefficiently doesn't make for a great mood in the morning when you're trying to get ready for the day. In fact, I started snoozing and needing a lot more coffee to be my peppy self. I also started complaining more, being more resentful and just not having the best time at work.

As a successful business owner, you need to start each day as if it's the most important day of your life. Your energy needs to be high. Your focus and dedication rock-solid. Why? Because anything less will negatively impact your employees. Yep. Your employees.

Your team looks to you to set the tone at your business. The whole concept of "leading by example" is real. If your tone is mopey and slightly on edge because you wake up and read negative emails first thing, it shouldn't be surprising that your team is mopey and slightly on edge as well. They take their cues from you.

So luckily, I stopped looking at my email when I got up. And started spending at least an hour reading business books or anything uplifting. Sometimes I listen to business podcasts. It was amazing. My mood improved. I didn't feel so rushed in the morning. And because I was operating with an improved outlook and mood—you guessed it—my team started working harder as well.

It never fails. I recently hit a small set-back in growing the business to a third location and because I was upset, our monthly sales took a dip. The next month, I resolved not to let this set-back affect my state of mind and we crushed it, for our best month of the year and beating our January sales by 5%.

If you are interested in furthering your success or even just getting on the right path to becoming more successful, I recommend reading the following:

The Compound Effect, Darren Hardy: This book literally changed my life. My business coach, Mary Ann, gave me a copy to read before one of our first meetings. Since reading the book, I cancelled my cable, started reading every day, enacted a strict budget both for my personal spending and business spending, and stopped going to Starbucks every day for coffee (I still drink coffee. And sometimes go to Starbucks. But I learned how to make a latte at home—that tastes just like Starbucks. It's really easy and I only had to spend $40 to get the right tools.) https://shesonhertoes. com/2016/11/18/how-to-make-a-latte-just-like-starbucks-at-home/

Anyways, back to The Compound Effect...this book is all about making small changes that "compound" to effect bigger more amazing changes. And it really works. If you are in the fitness industry you can attest, like I can, that just making one change to work out on a regular basis leads to making other smarter choices about food and drinking. Then all of a sudden, you've lost weight and people are commenting about how good you look. Anyways, get this book immediately, if not sooner. Read it. Implement just one suggestion—after all it's called The Compound Effect. See what happens.

The One Thing, Gary Keller: Along with The Compound Effect, this book also helped me turn my views on business ownership around. Keller explains that you are only capable of doing one thing at a time. There's no such thing as multitasking. And he should know, he built the biggest real estate company in the world from scratch, Keller Williams. Keller believes that in order to achieve success in work and life, you must find your "one thing." In other words, we've all been placed on this Earth to do one thing—and if you can narrow your focus to achieve it, you'll live an extraordinary life. Keller argues that "you can become successful with less discipline than you think, for one simple reason: success is about doing the right thing, not about doing everything right." Words to live by.

Success Principles, Jack Canfield: If you're going to read a book after The Compound Effect and The One Thing, read this one. Jack Canfield was the co-creator of the Chicken Soup for The Soul series.

In Success Principles, you will literally learn what the world's most successful people do and how to apply those principles to your own life. I need to read this book again. There was so much information. It's the kind of book that you could re-read many times and always pick up something new.

Think & Grow Rich, Napolean Hill: First published in 1937, this book is still applicable to today's modern business world. A must read.

The Little Red Book of Selling: Jeffrey Gittomer: Love, love, love this book. I learned two things from this book. 1) The workday starts the night before. In other words, you need to look at what you have planned for the next day to start mentally mapping out how your day will go. It works—if you have a plan and are mentally prepared, you win every time. 2) If you can't get in front of the decision maker to make the sale, you suck. Some of you might think this is harsh, but it's so true, it's not funny. If you are having trouble selling, either your product isn't what people want (aka. "it sucks") or you do.

The Edge: The Guide to Fulfilling Dreams, Maximizing Success and Enjoying a Lifetime of Achievement, Howard E. Ferguson: I first read this book in high school because my dad got a copy. And it really helped me stay focused to get up every morning for swim team (I lettered all four years and went on to swim in college). I don't even think this book is in print anymore, but you can buy used copies on Amazon. If you need a cliff notes of any of the books above, this is the book for you. This book is about getting "the edge" in life and it is comprised of quotes from anyone who was successful in sports, business, or politics. Disclaimer: this book was published in 1990, so there are quotes from OJ Simpson and Joe Paterno. Just pretend someone else said them.

When you're operating your own business, it's pretty easy to get bogged down in the day-to-day. Setting some time up to learn is critical so that you can have the confidence to grow your business and develop your team. I am convinced that 90% of successful business ownership is all between-the-ears. The other 10% is just planning and hard work. Meaning, if you're struggling, you've got to change your perspective and outlook on life. Get positive to have a positive impact on your sales. If you don't, your team will stagnate and you'll just lag behind your competition.

Determine What You Want

When you own a small business—hell even if you own a large business—every decision is important. We already discussed the importance of hiring the right team—critical. Your physical location, the appearance of your office, pricing, branding, marketing, whether or not you upgrade your toilet paper—all of these things add up to what your business is about and what clients you are trying to attract. When every decision is important, you don't want to make the "wrong" decision. And fear of making the "wrong" decision often leads to making no decision at all.

With the stakes so high, how is it possible to stay motivated to grow your business and also keep your employees focused on growing the business? Simple. All you have to do is ask yourself: "What do I want?"

Stay with me here...if you ask yourself "What do I want?" you'll have a vision for where you want to get in business or life, whatever. But if you don't have that vision, you won't get anywhere.

I once had a boss that said, "You should always know what your next job is before you even accept your current job." It was hard for me to understand the point he was trying to make because he would often get so angry at the office and yell at everyone that his nose would bleed. (I have since developed a slightly different management style—yelling without a bleeding nose. Less messy. Just kidding.) But after I stopped working for him, I actually realized what he was saying. You have to know your end point and make sure that every decision leads you in the direction of that final vision.

Ok. Great. I'll figure out what I want and that will keep me motivated to get there. Not quite. You'll want to take it one step further and create a Vision Board. Sounds a little silly, right? Wrong. Anyone can come up with conceptual goals and aspirations. But when you actually sit down, write them out or find pictures of what you want to create in your Vision Board, a funny thing starts to happen—they become real wants and your brain starts trying to solve all of the problems or obstacles preventing you from reaching those goals. What is a Vision Board anyway? It still sounds silly.

A Vision Board is a collection of images, words, or small trinkets that define your dreams and goals. I have one—I actually had one in high school without knowing it. I would tape cool pictures, magazine cutouts, and inspiring articles on my bedroom wall. I also wrote out quotes on the wall with a Sharpie—my Mom loved that. Every day I would read one or two and it helped me stay motivated to get up for swim team in the morning and go back to practice in the afternoon.

My Vision Board now is similar but it also has pictures of the kind of kitchen I want and places I want to travel—all things that I'm working towards by growing my business. Right now, do you see your business as a burden or series of problems dragging you down? Or do you look at your business as the vehicle you'll use to have fun and meaning in your life? Your Vision Board will help you refocus and get to the latter.

What's so interesting is that once you define your goals, they seem easier to reach. You'll stop coming up with excuses for trying to reach them and actually start working towards achieving them. You'll also be able to better direct your team at how to run your business. And nothing will be holding you back.

Learn to be Disciplined

As the business owner, you are responsible for motivating your team. Great. Got it. But what about motivating yourself? That's where things get a little tricky. How do you stay motivated when no one is at the top to motivate you?

Motivating yourself is an extremely difficult skill to hone. In fact, I'll go out on a limb here and say if you can't self-motivate, you probably shouldn't own your own business. If you have the skill of self-motivation, otherwise known as discipline, nothing can hold you back.

Once you've stepped up to be your own boss it can be lonely at the top. Instead of taking direction from a supervisor, you are setting the pace and direction at your business. And while controlling your own destiny can be incredibly freeing, it can also lead to doubts, uncertainty, and unfocused decisions.

Earlier I said that discipline is the hardest leadership skill to learn. The reason being is that it's the most boring and ungratifying.

It's easy to confuse motivation and discipline, but they are different. Motivation is the general desire or willingness to do something. Discipline occurs when you have determined the best course of action and follow that course regardless of your desire. Do you see the difference?

It's easy to be motivated when everything is going your way. Life is awesome, you're living the dream, motivation is high. Energy is high and working on your business is easy.

Discipline is on display when you don't want to do something, but do it anyway because you know it's the right thing. Fitness studio owners are already predisposed to discipline because how many times have you not wanted to work out but done it anyway because you knew you'd feel better or have an improved mood after a good sweat?

It's discipline that keeps you working on what you want from your business day after day, week after week, month after month, and ultimately year after year. And yes, that gets boring. It's also thankless and at times you will question whether you're on the right path or making the right decisions. This is where knowing what you want is so important. As long as you're working on things that will allow you to reach your established goal of what you want from your business, you're on the right path. But I think we've already established that owning a successful fitness studio isn't for everyone and requires a special set of skills.

Time Blocking

We've already established that it's important to get into the habit of setting yourself up for success each day and scheduling your time to reach your goals. But how do you stay disciplined when it can be so monotonous and tedious to do so?

Are you as into your to-do list has I am into mine? There's something so satisfying about checking off those to-do's. That sense of accomplishment makes you feel great about yourself.

But, have you ever stopped to think about whether the line items on your list are the "right" to-do's. Are your to-do's really helping you reach your goals? I mean, how many times have you already done something only to write it down on your list so you could check it off—100% guilty! You know you do it too.

The problem with to-do lists is that creating them doesn't usually take into account what you need to prioritize—or what you actually need to accomplish. The dark side of to-do's lies in their format which gives equal weight to each line item.

I bring this up because each of us have a lot to accomplish and we only have 24 hours in a day just like everyone else. So, the only way to get more done is to work smarter and prioritize.

How can you get more done in the same amount of time? Two words: time blocking.

The concept of time blocking is pretty simple. You create blocks of time to get your most important tasks completed first and then everything else gets done at the end of the day. Each night you also set aside a block of time to plan your next day and ensure your top priorities are actually tasks that will help you reach your broader goals. Planning the night before means that these top priorities are just in fact that—top priorities not just line items on a list.

If you get to the most important stuff first thing, you'll actually get it done. You won't run the risk of being sidetracked or getting tired in the afternoon and not finishing the things that are most important.

To work smarter, you'll have to build a better to-do list by making your to-do's things that are actually important and help you accomplish your goals. I've found that time blocking is the best way to stay disciplined and work towards your goals and doing what's most important to grow your business.

The key to business leadership success lies, in making an investment in yourself by attending seminars, reading books and learning from other business owners. The more you invest in your own leadership training, the more you can give back to your team. To succeed at owning a successful business, you must invest in your own leadership and management training and make it a continuous priority—there's that discipline again!

Notice that all of these things could easily be applied to succeed at owning an independent business or franchise alike. There's no secret sales strategy or silver bullet to franchise ownership or business success in general—sorry for the big let-down. It all boils down to knowing your numbers and operating your business within those means, creating your Company Culture and hiring only those who believe in it, and making it a priority to invest in your own leadership and management training.

Approaching business ownership by applying these three principles isn't sexy. It doesn't involve a killer Social Media plan or some cool video that goes viral. So maybe that's why more business owners don't jump at working on these things. If the foundation of your business isn't rock-solid, then you're going to keep struggling—whether you own a franchise or not.

How to stay on your toes:

In this chapter, I explained how to develop your leadership skills and stay self-motivated.

1. *What do you want from your business? In other words, what's your One Thing? How can you schedule your time to reach your goal?*
2. *What bad habits do you have that you could change to improve your attitude and lead by example for your employees?*
3. *Have you confused motivation and discipline in the past? What can you do going forward to stay disciplined?*

Conclusion

Owning a successful boutique fitness studio is all about making sound business decisions including hiring the right team, knowing how to motivate them, and investing in your own continuous leadership training. No MBA required. Really.

Throughout the pages of this book, we picked apart the following 5 problems just about every boutique fitness studio owner has encountered including:

1. **The perception that making money is "bad" in boutique fitness since making money is often associated with greed, miserly-ness and unjust corporate power—the opposite of the environment we're trying to create for our clients to enjoy when they come to take class or workout.**

   Bullshit: If you don't make money, you can't pay your rent, yourself or your employees and your studio can't stay open for your clients. We defined a fitness business as a "commercial, PROFITABLE enterprise that can be run without you so you can be a role model in the health and fitness community you are creating."

   Making money isn't a bad thing. Anytime I hear someone say the opposite, I think, "Good luck. Sounds like you're going to need it." There is honor in providing jobs in your community and growing your business to support growing your team and giving them more opportunity. There is also honor in providing an amazing fitness community dedicated to serving your clients by helping them to improve their health and strength.

2. **Lack of business experience or expertise. Many boutique fitness owners have no formal business training. They love the classes they teach and the studio environment. They are great teachers, but don't know how to run a business.**

I think I've established that even with an MBA, you can make terrible decisions and almost lose your business. Hitting rock bottom can happen to anyone—it did to me. Awesome. Not inspiring?

Ok. Ok. Following business fundamentals doesn't require a fancy degree. It's also important to surround yourself with a sounding board—the people who hold you accountable for all your business decisions, like a financial planner, an accountant and a business coach.

3. **Lack of leadership experience. Many owners don't know how to motivate employees or teach them how to sell.**

In Chapter 7, I gave you my five most compelling ways to motivate my team. Hopefully you can use these to get started motivating your employees to achieve great things.

4. **Most employees are part-time, dis-engaged and lack business savvy. Many boutique fitness employees**

float from job-to-job and often don't stay at the studio long-term.

If you take anything away from this book, I hope that it's not good enough to simply hire employees for your business. You have to take the time to hire the RIGHT employees for your business. I detailed my hiring process in Chapter 6. I hope you'll read through the worksheets to develop your own Vision, Mission and Culture Statements so you spend your time hiring only those people who support your business goals and values.

5. **Since teaching and taking class literally requires the owner to work to exhaustion, finding time to work on the business is difficult or limited.**

Each chapter of the book comes back to solving this problem. If you hire a great team you'll give yourself more time to work on your business. If you're not working yourself to exhaustion and working as the leader of your fitness community, you can create more thoughtful and targeted marketing campaigns to generate leads and improve retention. In addition, you'll also have more time to become a better leader and give your team more support. It's all one big circle—you support your team so they can support your clients and your clients support your studio, which supports you and your team.

Serial Entrepreneur

This book is the result of my 5-year journey through business ownership. It all started with leaving a lucrative job in investment banking and taking a chance that I could live a more fulfilled life if I were my own boss operating a business that I was truly passionate about. It has been a roller coaster ride complete with the highest of highs and the lowest of lows.

Would I do it again? You're damn right I would!

I started a business, expanded it, almost lost it and got back up on my toes. And all without any grey hair—although that's probably due to superior hair genetics. Thanks Dad!

In all seriousness, one of the highlights of my business journey was winning an award for my success at an ActionCOACH conference. When you become your own boss, there aren't that many times—if any—that you'll be recognized or celebrated for your accomplishments. And winning the Best Serviced-Based Business with over 10 employees was especially meaningful because I was chosen to win by Sir Winston Churchill's great grandson. Oh yeah, that guy was pretty cool. Got to talk to him after. We're friends on Facebook now. But as one of the most prolific leaders of the 20th Century or ever, Churchill once said, "Success is not final, failure is not fatal, it is the courage to continue that counts." And continue I will.

So, what's next for me? What's my next goal or dream? I have come to realize that while I am a business owner, I'm also a professional problem-solver. There are many more challenges for me to tackle and problems left to solve at my studios. And I would love to solve them all—but I'm not going to.

Instead, I'm going to continue to train my team to solve them for me.

My next goal is to become a serial entrepreneur and start another business. I hope you'll continue to follow my next journey in business as I chronicle my path on my website and blog She's on Her Toes (www.shesonhertoes.com).

Two Words, Big Message

As I mentioned earlier, there is no better time for a woman to own her own business especially if that business is in fitness. If you are struggling to hire good employees, motivate your existing team, keep yourself on task, and increase your profits, you aren't alone. Every business owner struggles and faces challenges each day they are open. Even those business owners you think have it all figured out have problems. They do. Trust me.

The difference between being successful in business and going down in a blaze of glory lies in the fact that successful business owners know their strengths and take the time to cultivate them—they invest in themselves and work to be better leaders and they hire employees who compensate for their weaknesses.

I personally am not into details. I come up with ideas, but I don't care how they are implemented as long as they are. Not always the best way to manage a group of 20 team members who might need more information. My solution, hire a manager who is great at the details. In fact, she has so many notebooks and folders going, I don't know how she keeps track of them all. But that's the point! I do what I do best and she does what she does best.

Successful business owners create a plan and have the discipline to keep at it day-after-day, week-after-week, year-after-year. In other words, they outlast their competition by working on the fundamentals and not chasing after the latest, fad or unproven concept. They know they have a good service or product and can provide excellent customer service to keep their clients coming back for more. They just don't quit.

I'll share with you a poem that I've read hundreds of times. While there is no known author to attribute these powerful words, I first read it in the pages of **The Edge: The Guide to Fulfilling Dreams, Maximizing Success and Enjoying a Lifetime of Achievement**, a book I recommended in Chapter 9. I hope you find as much meaning in it as I have, and that these words encourage you to keep working towards your own dreams.

Don't Quit

When things go wrong as they sometimes will,
When the road you're trudging seems all uphill,
When the funds are low and the debts are high,
And you want to smile, but you have to sigh,
When care is pressing you down a bit—
Rest if you must, but don't you quit.

Life is queer with its twists and turns,
As every one of us sometimes learns,
And many a person turns about
When they might have won had they stuck it out.
Don't give up though the pace seems slow—
You may succeed with another blow.

Often the struggler has given up
When he might have captured the victor's cup;
And he learned too late when the night came down,
How close he was to the golden crown.

Success is failure turned inside out—
So stick to the fight when you're hardest hit,—
It's when things seem worst that you mustn't quit.

All the best!

Carolyn

98120138R00063

Made in the USA
Lexington, KY
04 September 2018